MUSLIM
WRITERS

PUBLISHING

Serving Up Faith

Recipes
Cooking Tips
Inspirational Stories

Muslim Writers Publishing
Tempe, Arizona

Disclaimers:
Articles and external links published in this book do not necessarily represent the views of Muslim Writers Publishing or the Islamic Writers Alliance Inc. None of the content of this book is intended to be taken as medical or nutritional advice. Muslim Writers Publishing and the Islamic Writers Alliance Inc. are not responsible for any health issues which may arise from the usage of any ingredients written about in this book. Medical professionals should be consulted for any serious illness.

Muslim Writers Publishing
PO Box 27632
Tempe, Arizona 85285
USA

ISBN: 978-0-9819770-7-2

Cover Art by Balqees Mohammed
Editing by Balqees Mohammed
Book Design by Leila Joiner

Printed in the United States of America

BismAllah

Introduction

IWA – Who We Are

The Islamic Writers Alliance, Inc. is a United States-based, tax exempt, non-profit, professional Muslim organization with an international membership. Members include published and aspiring writers, editors, artists, publishers, journalists, playwrights, web designers, retailers, and marketing consultants. The IWA is an inclusive organization and welcomes adult Muslim men and women of all races, ethnicities, linguistic backgrounds, abilities, and creeds. The purpose of the IWA is the promotion of literacy worldwide and the promotion and support of the organization and its membership.

IWA – What We Do

In furthering its purpose the IWA has established some specific goals. The IWA promotes Islamic fiction books and authors, regularly awards fiction and non-fiction Islamic books to Islamic school libraries and sponsors creative writing contests for Islamic schools. The IWA sponsors an annual public poetry contest and an annual public Islamic fiction story contest.

The IWA also publishes a quarterly online IWA Magazine, which showcases the work of the IWA membership. IWA has three published print books: *Many Voices, One Faith* published in 2004 and *Many Voices, One Faith II – Islamic Fiction Stories* and *Many Poetic Voices, One Faith* – both published in 2009.

Our Newest Book

Serving Up Faith: Recipes – Cooking Tips – Inspirational Stories is our newest and the fourth IWA book to be published.

The purpose for publishing this new book is to help the organization raise money from the sales of the book to use to help fund the literacy projects we complete each year.

Serving Up Faith includes 84 halal recipes from many parts of the world, all of which were donated by members and their families and friends. This unique book also attempts to nourish the spirit as well as the body with the inclusion of some of our members' conversion and finding faith again stories. We have included a dozen beneficial articles that will give the readers some beneficial cooking do's and don'ts. We sincerely hope your mind, body, and spirit will benefit from the content on the pages within the covers of this special book.

Special Thanks

The Islamic Writers Alliance gives a special thank you to the Zakat Foundation of America for providing its support for our cookbook, *Serving Up Faith*.

Zakat Foundation of America (ZF) is an international charity organization that helps generous and caring people reach out to those in need. Our goal is to address immediate needs and ensure the self-reliance of the poorest people around the world with Zakat and Sadaqa dollars of privileged Muslims and the support of other generous donors. We believe that those whom God has granted wealth need to cleanse that wealth through charity, and those whom God has tried with loss are accorded a rightful share from the resources of the affluent.

Mission: ZF fosters charitable giving to alleviate the immediate needs of poor communities and to establish long-term development projects that ensure individual and community growth.

- Bringing immediate relief during and after disasters, building and supporting schools, orphanages and health clinics, supporting community development programs and micro-credit, providing Ramadan Iftars and food distribution, and providing fresh meat for Udhiya/Qurbani and Aqeeqah through the support of community-based initiatives

- Serving as a trusted Zakat and Sadaqa resource center for our Muslim donors

- Serving as a trusted charity option for all donors through financial transparency and strict standards of efficiency and accountability

- Minimizing expenses by maintaining a small administrative staff

- Maximizing donations by establishing strategic partnerships

History

- ZF was founded in 2001 upon the Islamic principle illustrated in the Gracious Quran:

  "They feed with food--despite their own desire for it-- the indigent, and the orphan and the captive (saying): 'We feed you purely for the sake of God. We desire no reward from you, nor thankfulness.'" — *Surah al-Insan 8-9*

- ZF was established during a time when humanitarian organizations faced increased scrutiny in their activities and procedures, leading to new standards in transparency and accountability. As a US-based, Muslim-run charity organization that serves needy communities both at home and abroad, ZF shows the inclusive beauty of Islam through programs that reach the destitute worldwide.

- ZF has differentiated itself from a traditional US-based Muslim charity approach of exclusively supporting communities abroad and reaches poor and indigent communities within the United States as well. Since its establishment, ZF has progressed from mostly offering immediate emergency aid and Seasonal Programs to a focus on severing the roots of poverty, utilizing Zakat and Sadaqa donations to develop long-term, sustainable solutions. Zakat Foundation of America at www.zakat.org.

Serving Up Faith

Recipes

Cooking Tips

Inspirational Stories

Islamic Writers Alliance, Inc.

Table of Contents

Section I – Recipes

Soups & Salads

Lissan Asfour Soup, Egyptian Style
– Judith Nelson Eldawy

Ingredients

A package of orzo pasta
1 tbsp. of butter
1-2 tbsp. of extra virgin olive oil
Stock-chicken or beef
Lemon wedges

Method

1. Melt butter and add olive oil to a medium sized saucepan pan.

2. Add orzo pasta. To make soup for 4-6 people, use about half a package or 1 cup. You can reduce or increase this amount very easily. Be aware that the pasta will absorb liquid and swell even after browning.

3. Brown pasta in butter and olive oil. This will take about 2-3 minutes, depending on desired browning.

4. Add stock to fill pan and be sure to get bits of the onion, tomato and garlic. Be careful because ladling stock into the pan will cause a huge cloud of steam to rise very quickly.

5. Boil on medium heat for about 10 to 15 minutes.

Serve with lemon wedges to be squeezed into broth directly before eating.

Quaker Soup
– Balqees Mohammed

Quaker Soup is a traditional soup made any time of the year, but most popular served at the breakfast during the month of fasting, Ramadan.

It is most generally called 'Quaker Soup' because of one of the main ingredients: Quaker Instant Oats. But there are many other ingredients, each one special and necessary to the soup in their own rites. Good served at lunch or evening dinner with plain bread, sandwiches or even samboosa. * Also an excellent quick energy dish served at the meal either at the time of the sunset breakfast during the month of Ramadan, when Muslims fast, or at the meal served immediately after the sunset prayers which are performed after the initial official breaking of the fast daily.

Ingredients

¼ lb. meat (chicken breasts lamb or beef) cut into 1" chunks

1 medium red onion, chopped finely

2-6 garlic sections, chopped finely

2-4 medium or large very red/ripe tomatoes, puréed in blender

1 cube bouillon or chicken broth

¼ cup vermicelli (or other small macaroni-stars, alphabet, etc.)

1 tbsp. tomato paste

2 qt. water

1 cup Instant Quaker Oats

1 tsp. ground cinnamon (or two large pieces cinnamon bark)

Salt & pepper to taste

2 tbsp. cooking oil

1 chili pepper

1 cup whole barley (optional)

1 lemon, quartered, for serving

Parsley for garnish

Method

1. Use a deep saucepan, large enough to accommodate the amount of soup you desire, allowing for room for boiling.

2. Heat the oil in the saucepan until it starts to become bubbly.

3. Add the chopped onion and garlic.

4. Stir consistently until the chopped onion becomes clear and the garlic begins to brown. At this point, add the meat.

5. Stir the meat in the onion/garlic/oil mixture.

6. When the meat begins to change color on the outside, then add the pureed tomatoes, allowing this to simmer well on full heat until most of the moisture of the tomatoes has evaporated. Continue stirring so the mixture doesn't stick or burn.

7. Add the tomato paste, spices (cinnamon, chili pepper, and salt & pepper), the chicken bouillon cube or broth, and the water.

8. Also add the barley (if you are using it) and vermicelli (or other macaroni) at this time.

9. Let this mixture come to a full boil, and then turn down slightly so as to prevent spilling over while cooking, but to allow for a continuous boil. If you are using a pressure cooker, close it tightly and time your food for cooking the meat till well done (depending upon the area you are in, anywhere from 15-20 minutes should be enough). Otherwise, watch it as it cooks, being cautious so as to remove it before any burning may occur, or adding additional liquid as needed.

10. Once the meat has cooked add the Quaker Instant Oats. Be careful that the oats do not bunch up into clogs, so flake them in, stirring the soup quickly with a whisk as you do this, to ensure that it mixes well immediately with the liquid as you add it.

11. Let simmer for a few moments, until the soup thickens. If it becomes too thick you can add more water, and if the soup is too thin, you can add more oats.

12. Serve hot from the stove with lemon wedges on the side.

Optional - You can pick off sprigs of the parsley and lay on the top of the soup bowl as garnish, or chop the parsley finely and sprinkle over the top. Either way, the parsley makes a colorful as well as tasty garnish for any soup.

Always a good choice served with bread, sandwiches, samboosa, spring rolls, or served alone.

Note - If you opt to include whole barley in your soup, soak it well in warm water from the time you begin preparation (cutting, etc.) of the ingredients. This will help in the cooking of this ingredient, as it takes long to get the whole barley well done-sometimes longer than the meat itself. The whole barley is not necessary for this soup, but it is an extra addition of flavor and texture, as well as of course nutritious.

*Samboosa is a pastry filled with a mixture of minced meat or minced chicken combined with chopped green onions and parsley. The complete filled pastry is usually deep-fried, but can be baked in the oven, as per preference. It is a traditional favorite for Muslims in the Middle East to be served at any meal throughout the year, but most popular at the meal of the breakfast at sunset during the month of fasting: Ramadan.

Onion Soup with Black Seed Oil
– Amina Malik

All of these ingredients are known to fight a multitude of illnesses but this soup is ideal when you have a cold. The onions contain sulphur, which helps combat cold symptoms, the ginger is a natural anti-inflammatory and the garlic and coriander are antibiotics. Black seed oil is a cure for every disease. Although bitter tasting, combined in this soup, it is an excellent cure for a cold.

Eating this soup when you are well will boost your immune system and protect against illness.

Ingredients

2½ oz. butter

4 cups yellow onions, sliced finely

2 sprigs of thyme

A pinch of salt

2½ cups l chicken stock (either home-made or use good quality stock cubes)

½ cup sliced mushrooms

1 tsp. ground coriander

2 cloves of garlic sliced finely

2 chunks of ginger sliced finely

¼ cup double cream

1 tsp. freshly ground pepper

4 tbsp. pure black seed oil

Method

1. Slice onions thinly.

2. Melt butter in a saucepan over a gentle heat

3. Add the onions, thyme and a pinch of salt. Cook for 30 minutes with the lid on the pan, allowing the onions to become soft but not brown. Stir the contents now and again to ensure the onions do not stick to the pan.

4. Pour in the stock and then turn up the heat to medium.

5. Add the mushrooms, coriander, garlic and ginger and leave to simmer for 25 minutes.

6. Once cooked, blitz with a hand blender until mostly smooth. Stir in cream and leave until serving.

7. When ready to serve, re-heat gently but do not boil. Add ground pepper to the top.

8. In each bowl, drizzle 1tbsp black seed oil just before serving.

Note - it is important not to cook the black seed oil as its health benefits may be reduced if exposed to very high temperatures.

Definition - Pure black seed oil refers to virgin pressed oil, with no other added ingredients.

The Holy Qur'an 6:99 It is He Who sendeth down rain from the skies: with it We produce vegetation of all kinds: from some We produce green (crops), out of which We produce grain, heaped up (at harvest); out of the date-palm and its sheaths (or spathes) (come) clusters of dates hanging low and near: and (then there are) gardens of grapes, and olives, and pomegranates, each similar (in kind) yet different (in variety): when they begin to bear fruit, feast your eyes with the fruit and the ripeness thereof. Behold! In these things there are signs for people who believe.

Harira
– Anisa Abeytia

I love this soup and I have yet to meet someone who turned his or her nose up at it. Traditionally this is what Moroccans break their fast with. The meal goes on after that, but when served with nice whole grain bread, it is more than enough as a complete meal. It is nourishing, easily digested, hydrating and has to be one of the most perfect Ramadan foods, besides dates.

Ingredients

½ lb. boneless lamb, cut into very fine bits

1 can chickpeas, drained

1 ½ cups red lentils

1 onion, peeled and diced

1 60 oz. can Roma tomatoes, diced and peeled

1 bunch cilantro, diced

1 bunch Italian parsley, diced

A pinch of saffron, crushed

1-2 tbsp. ground cinnamon

¼ tsp. ground ginger

3-4 tbsp. tomato paste

3 tbsp. coconut oil

¼ cup vermicelli noodles

3 quarts water

1 strip of kombu (seaweed)

Salt

Lemon to serve

Method

1. Heat a pot and add in the coconut oil.
2. Add in the onions, lamb and a pinch of salt and brown.
3. Add in the spices and fry for 1 minute.
4. Add in the chickpeas, red lentils, tomatoes, kombu, and a pinch of salt.
5. Pour in 3 quarts of water.
6. Bring to a boil and turn down to medium heat, cover and cook for 1 hour.
7. Add in the vermicelli, cilantro, parsley, tomato paste and a pinch of salt.
8. If you would like the soup to be thicker, add in more tomato paste.
9. Turn heat to low and allow to cook for 20 minutes before adding salt to taste.
10. Serve with lemon wedges and dates.

Lentil Soup
– Balqees Mohammed

As with anything of the legume family, this soup made essentially of
lentil beans is an excellent vegetarian substitute for protein. It is also a
nice light yet filling soup for any meal, but in particular for the meal taken after breaking the
fast during the month of Ramadan. Nice along with some fresh baked bread, sandwiches
or samboosa, or fine alone on its own.

Ingredients

2 cups split lentils (either green or red)

8 cups clear chicken broth (or two cubes of bouillon and 8 cups water)

1 medium sized onion, diced

2 cloves garlic, diced very fine or crushed

1 tbsp. vegetable oil

1 tsp. salt

1 tsp. pepper

For garnish:

6 sprigs parsley

1 lemon cut in wedges or slices

Method

1. Prepare the lentils by removing all excess debris (stones, chaff, etc.) and cleansing thoroughly.

2. In a saucepan large enough to accommodate the measurement of liquid (2 quarts), sauté the onions and garlic.

3. Add the broth (or water and bouillon cubes), and let it come to a boil.

4. After first stirring and rinsing the lentils one more time, drain well before adding to the boiling broth mixture. Add pepper. Taste the broth first before adding salt. Add salt only if the broth is terribly bland.

5. Stirring frequently to ward off possible burning of the lentils at the bottom of the pan, continue to boil on high temperature for about 1-2 minutes.

6. Turn the heat down to a low medium, and let simmer until the lentils are fully cooked. This will result in a heavier texture of soup than the previous liquidly broth, and the lentils will no longer retain their previous round appearance. The final consistency should be similar to the consistency of any heavy cream soup. If it is too thick, add some more broth or water, and stir to mix well. If it is too thin, let simmer more to cook out some of the excess water, resulting in a more thick soup.

This soup mixture should serve approximately four. Garnish the tops of each separate bowl with finely diced parsley. Place lemon wedges or slices on the plate beside the soup bowl.

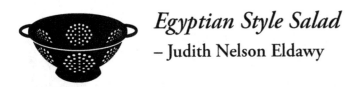

Egyptian Style Salad
– Judith Nelson Eldawy

Ingredients

3-4 Tomatoes

3-4 Cucumbers

1 medium Onion

Fresh coriander and dill - leaves, not stems

Salt

Black pepper

Cumin

Vinegar

Fresh lemon or lime juice

Water - a few tablespoons

Method

1. Dice all vegetables.
2. Add seasonings to taste.
3. Add water and squeeze the juice of one lemon or lime into salad.

You can add carrot or peppers, but you will never see lettuce in an Arab salad. Lettuce, watercress, and other leafy salad greens are washed and eaten either alone or with bread for breakfast or late night suppers.

Molokhiya
– Green Leaf Vegetable

Ingredients

1¾ cups of broth (meat or chicken)

1½ tsp. garlic

2 tsp. ground Coriander (Kozbara)

3 tbsp. tomato paste (tomato paste is optional, but preferable)

1½ tbsp. butter (or 2 tablespoons of oil)

Salt and black pepper

The Molokhiya, green, dry or frozen

Method

1. Add the Molokhiya (one bag) to the 1¾ cups of soup.
2. Heat for about 15 minutes on medium heat.

Note - It is not recommended to stir too much, so the Molokhiya doesn't drain in the bottom. (In case of green Molokhiya, not dry.)

Serves 3-4

Grilled Chicken and Walnut Salad

Ingredients

3 boneless, skinless grilled chicken breasts (chopped and shredded) or
  (2) 5 oz. cans of breast of chicken

½ cup fat-free mayonnaise

1 tbsp. Dijon or Creole mustard

⅓ cup halved seedless red grapes

½ cup chopped walnuts

2 tbsp. Cajun spice or one each of salt and pepper

½ stalk finely chopped celery (optional)

Method

1. First, chop and shred the chicken breasts leaving some chunky pieces or place the canned chicken into a large bowl.

2. Combine chicken, mayo, and Dijon mustard and mix until chicken is fully coated and consistency is even.

3. Add spice, celery, walnuts and grapes and stir in evenly.

4. Serve on a sandwich or bed of lettuce and enjoy! Variation: you could also add chopped red pepper for extra flavor!

This wonderful lunch treat is great on toasted rye or served on a lush bed of lettuce!

Cranberry-Apple Crunch

Ingredients

2 cups of coarsely cut red apples. Remove the stems, cores and seeds

4 stalks of crisp celery coarsely cut into medium bite-sized pieces

1 tbsp. of lemon juice

1 medium sized package of dried cranberries, no preservatives added

½ cup of cashews, halved

Method

1. Cut the apples and place them in a medium size bowl.
2. Drizzle the lemon juice over the apple pieces.
3. Cut the celery and add to the apple pieces and mix lightly.
4. Add the package of dried cranberries and cashews and lightly mix.
5. Cover the bowl and store in the refrigerator until ready to serve.

The Holy Qur'an 60:4 "Our Lord! In You we have placed our trust, and to You do we turn in repentance, for unto You is the end of all journeys."

Green Pea Salad

Ingredients

6 tbsp. white vinegar

½ cup vegetable or olive oil

¼ tsp. black pepper

½ tbsp. water

½ cup sugar

Method

1. Mix ingredients and heat to boiling in a small pan.

2. Let the mixture cool and pour over vegetable ingredients listed below. Serve at room temperature.

Vegetable Ingredients

¼ cup finely chopped onion

1 medium can of green peas

1 tsp. salt

1 red bell pepper cut in small pieces

1 cup of coarsely chopped celery

Algerian Salad

– Leigha Hoffner

Ingredients

2 sweet red peppers, seeded and chopped fine

4 medium ripe tomatoes, chopped

¾ cup sliced cucumber

2 small onions, sliced thin

½ cup black olives, pitted and halved

6 anchovy fillets, chopped

2 hard-boiled eggs, quartered

1 tsp. chopped fresh basil or cilantro

3 tbsp. olive oil

1 tbsp. vinegar

Salt and pepper to taste

Method

Place all ingredients into a large salad bowl and toss gently.

May be served with pita bread.

Carrot Salad
– Amina Malik

Choosing a Carrot Salad is a great way to boost your 5 a day vegetable intake – and trick the kids into eating healthily! Simple yet delicious, this salad is a great side dish. The longer you leave it to absorb the mayonnaise the tastier this salad is. Make in the morning and then refrigerate until dinnertime.

Ingredients

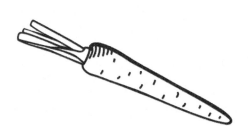

2 carrots

½ red pepper

½ cucumber

¼ cup of cooked sweet corn

1 large tomato

2 tbsp. mayonnaise

Method

1. Peel and grate the carrots

2. Chop the pepper, cucumber and tomato and mix into the carrots

3. Add the sweet corn

4. Stir in the mayonnaise

Optional - Add lemon juice for a kick to the flavour

Serves two.

Children's Chicken Noodle Soup

– Linda D. Delgado

Children love chicken noodle soup. My kids always complained that the chicken noodle soup from a can hardly had any chicken in it. So I began to make this soup for them. Many children don't like to have their foods mixed and some will look at a new food suspiciously. This recipe keeps the soup plain and simple while providing a healthy food they will want to eat. Adding a fun Veggie Pal or Fruit Carousel will provide a well-balanced meal. Having fun with food helps to make eating a good experience for children and carries forward into their teen years.

Ingredients

1 medium or large whole chicken – the size of the chicken will be determined by the number to be served

1 or 2 packages of wide egg noodles or no-yokes noodles

Salt to taste

Water to cook the chicken

Method

1. Rinse the chicken thoroughly and place in a large pot.

2. Fill the pot ¾ full with water and add salt to taste.

3. Cover the pot but leave the lid partially open to allow the steam to escape to keep the water in the pot from boiling over.

4. Cook the chicken on medium heat until the meat is about ready to fall off the bones.

5. Remove the chicken from the pot and place on a large plate or cookie sheet to cool off. I remove the skin and bones while the chicken is hot as it is easier to do this at this time as well.

6. When the chicken is cool enough to handle, have your kids help you debone it completely. I always let my kids tear the chicken into pieces. Naturally they slip a few chicken pieces into their mouths and I kid with them telling them to stop pick 'in on my chick 'in.

7. The broth left from cooking the chicken should have cooled enough to skim the chicken fat from the surface. ⇨

8. Do this before adding the chunks of chicken back into the broth and then adding the egg noodles.

9. Cook the noodles until ready for serving. I immediately pour the chicken and noodle soup into a large bowl so the noodles will not continue cooking from the heat of the pot.

The Prophet also quoted God as saying: "O son of Adam, I asked you for food and you fed Me not." God was then asked: "O Lord, how should I feed You when You are the Lord of the worlds?" In reply, God said: "Did you not know that My (servant) asked you for food and you fed him not? Did you not know that had you fed him, you would surely have found (the reward for doing so) with Me?" (Hadith Qudsi 18)

Children's Veggie Pal

– Linda D. Delgado

Ingredients

1 large tomato sliced horizontally to make tomato circles

2 to 4 medium pitted black olives

1 or 2 hard-boiled eggs, sliced vertically to make egg ovals

4 to 8 walnut halves (walnuts are a heart-healthy nut)

X number of pieces of the green leafy lettuce from a head of lettuce. The number of pieces you need will depend on the number of children you will be serving.

1 package of small sized or "baby" carrots; 2 carrot sticks per Veggie Pal

1 package of sprouts

2 celery stalks cut into 1 inch lengths. Be sure the pieces are not wide, as they will become the arms of the Veggie Pal.

Small dinner plates or paper plates

1 toothpick

A dab of mayo

Method

Assembling the Veggie Pal

1. Flatten a piece of lettuce on the plate and place one tomato slice in the center of it.

2. You can leave it plain or drizzle your child's favorite salad dressing on the lettuce and tomato.

3. At the top of the tomato slice place one slice of egg horizontally.

4. Place some sprouts around the top of the egg (hair).

5. Place celery stick on each side of the tomato (arms) with a walnut piece at the lower end of the celery stick (hands).

6. Place two carrot sticks at the bottom of the tomato (legs) with a walnut piece at the end of each carrot stick (feet).

7. Cut an olive in half and place on either side of the egg (head), which will become the Veggie Pal's ears.

8. With a small amount of mayo at the end of a toothpick draw two eyes and a big smile on the yoke of the egg.

Children's Fruit Carousel
– Linda D. Delgado

A Fruit Carousel is the perfect complement for a children's meal that includes Children's Chicken Noodle Soup and a Veggie Pal. I had a picky eater and found that making the food fun to look at and eat went a long way to getting my picky eater to enjoy different foods.

Ingredients

1 or 2 red apples depending on the number of children to be served

½ cup red seedless grapes

½ cup green seedless grapes

½ cup whole strawberries

½ cup walnut halves

1 or 2 bananas depending on how many children will be served

1 small box (individual size) raisins

1 can of pineapple chunks

1 orange or tangelo

½ cup pistachios

1 box of toothpicks

1 package of small paper party plates

Multiple-colored cake decoration pieces, usually found in the cake and icing section of a grocery store. The colored pieces are packaged in small plastic containers and are usually sprinkled on cookies or cakes.

¼ cup lemon juice

Prep Work

1. Wash all the fresh fruits and dry before beginning assembly of the Fruit Carousel.

2. Cut the apple so the pieces are circular in shape and remove the center core.

3. Brush each side of the apple slices with lemon juice to keep the apples from turning brown.

4. Cut the banana into circular pieces.

5. Drain the pineapple chunks and set the chunks aside.

6. Peel the orange, remove the skin of the orange slices, and cut each slice in 2 or 3 pieces depending on the size of the slice.

Method

1. Place one apple slice in the center of a party paper plate.

2. Using six toothpicks place fruit pieces on the toothpicks as you would if making a kebab. You can place one kind of fruit only on a toothpick or you can mix up the combination of fruit pieces.

3. Leave enough room at the top and bottom of the toothpicks to be able to stick them in the bottom apple slice and the top apple slice you will place as the top of the carousel.

4. On the top of the bottom of the carousel place pieces of walnut; on the top of the carousel sprinkle the multi-colored cake/cookie decorations.

5. In the center of the bottom slice of apple (bottom of the carousel) fill with pistachios.

Children's Potato Salad
– Linda D. Delgado

Ingredients

3 white Idaho style potatoes, boiled in their skins until cooked but firm

3 large eggs, hardboiled

1 medium can whole pitted black olives

Miracle Whip Light Salad Dressing; quantity needed to cover
potato/egg/olive mixture

1 tbsp. yellow mustard

Method

1. Boil potatoes, but do not peel them until after they are cooked and cooled to at least room temperature. They will be easier to dice if you place them in the refrigerator for an hour or two.

2. Boil eggs and peel them after they have cooled to room temperature.

3. Mix the diced potatoes, eggs and olives in a bowl.

4. Add salt to taste.

5. Add Miracle Whip Salad Dressing to the mixture. The eggs, potatoes and olives should be covered.

6. Finally add the mustard to give the salad some color.

7. Chill before serving.

Note - Add one potato and one egg for each additional serving. Secret: Be sure to use the Miracle Whip salad dressing and not mayonnaise. Most kids don't like mayonnaise, but do like the salad dressing. They also like to poke their fingers into the whole, pitted olives.

Adult Version - Add ½ diced onion, ½ cup chopped celery, parsley, 1 tbsp. cumin, and black pepper to taste.

Tabbouleh

– Balqees Mohammed

Tabbouleh, or Parsley Salad, is a traditional appetizer of the *sham* region of Arabia: that is, it traditionally originates from Lebanon, Syria and Jordan. It has developed into a highly popular inclusion on menus for nearly all restaurants in any region of the Arabian countries, regardless of the specialty of that restaurant. Word has it that parsley is a particularly excellent natural remedy to try to ward off the development (or to lower, if already afflicted) of high concentrations of uric acid in the blood, which results in painful joints, in particular those of the toes and knees. Perhaps this is the reason that it is usually the most popular entry requested when people order dishes of barbecue meats at the restaurants.

Ingredients

2 cups green flat-leaf parsley, chopped very fine

4-5 green onions, chopped fine (chop the whole onion – both the white end as well as the green shoots)

1 medium sized ripe (but not soft) tomato

½ cup white burghul

1 lemon

1 tbsp. olive oil

Salt (to taste – approximately ½ to 1 tsp.)

Method

1. Measure out the burghul into a small bowl, and cover with water (about twice the depth of the burghul). Let soak for about 5-10 minutes, or until softened when squeezed. Pour the burghul and water into a small-opening sieve, and set sieve with remaining burghul on top of a larger bowl to continue draining excess water.

2. Finely chop both the parsley and green onions.

3. Finely dice the tomato, reserving about 1 tbsp. in a separate dish.

4. Squeeze the lemon and run juice through a small sieve to remove any remnant seeds.

5. Put all of the above ingredients, except for the reserved diced tomato, together in a bowl large enough to accommodate easy mixing. At this stage, add the olive oil and salt to taste. (Always best to start with a very small measurement of salt. You can always add more if needed.)

6. The salad can be served in the mixing bowl with serving spoon for everyone to dish out their desired amount, or on separate dishes for each individual or section of the table. ⇨

7. Garnish the top with the remaining diced tomato by simply placing it on the top in the center. Can also be garnished with several small leaves of romaine lettuce standing upright placed throughout, and using the larger green leaves as a bed in the serving plate/bowl. Lemon wedges or slices are also a nice garnish for this dish.

The Holy Qur'an: 2:25 But give glad tidings to those who believe and work righteousness, that their portion is Gardens, beneath which rivers flow. Every time they are fed with fruits therefrom, they say: "Why, this is what we were fed with before," for they are given things in similitude; and they have therein Companions pure and holy; and they abide therein forever.

The Holy Qur'an 16:14 It is He Who has made the sea subject, that ye may eat thereof flesh that is fresh and tender, and that ye may extract therefrom ornaments to wear; and thou seest the ships therein that plough the waves, that ye may seek (thus) of the bounty of Allah and that ye may be grateful.

Main Dishes

Lasagna Egyptian Style
– Dr. Freda Shamma

Egyptians are famous for their *macaroni beshamel*, macaroni with a white sauce. From the time I married my Egyptian husband I enjoyed this dish. However as someone who really enjoys Italian food, over the years I have combined lasagna with macaroni beshamel to create a family favorite.

Ingredients

9 uncooked lasagna noodles

Ground beef mixture:

½ lb. extra lean ground beef

3 large cloves garlic, finely chopped

1 onion, finely chopped

1 small can tomato sauce

½ cup water

1 tsp. Italian seasoning

White Sauce

7 cups 2% milk

9 tbsp. cornstarch

1 cup water

¼ cup olive oil

2 eggs

2 cups reduced fat ricotta cheese

2 cups shredded reduced-fat mozzarella cheese (8 oz.)

1/3 cup shredded Parmesan cheese

Salt to taste

Method

1. Cook noodles according to directions, drain, and place in cold water.
2. Cook beef, onion and garlic in a skillet with 1-tablespoon oil over medium-high heat 5 to 7 minutes, stirring frequently, until beef is thoroughly cooked.
3. Stir in tomato sauce, ½ cup water, Italian seasoning and salt to taste.
4. Heat to boiling, stirring occasionally.
5. Remove from heat.

White Sauce Method

1. Mix cornstarch in ¾ cup water, and continue to add water until the mix is the consistency of thin gravy. ⇨

2. Meanwhile, heat the milk in a large saucepan until bubbles begin to appear.

3. Using a wire whisk, add in the cornstarch mixture and olive oil, and stir constantly for about 5 minutes until the sauce is the consistency of gravy. (This requires constant attention or the sauce will burn on the bottom of the pan.)

4. Remove from heat and add salt.

5. Heat oven to 350°F. In medium bowl, beat 1 egg slightly.

6. Stir in ricotta cheese.

7. Drain noodles.

8. Grease bottom and sides of 13x9-inch glass baking dish.

9. Spread about ½ cup sauce mixture over bottom of baking dish.

10. Top with 3 noodles, half of meat mixture, half of the ricotta mixture and ¾ cup of the mozzarella cheese.

11. Repeat layers once. Top with remaining noodles.

12. Add 1 beaten egg and the remaining mozzarella cheese to the remaining white sauce.

13. Cover the top layer of noodles with this mixture, and then sprinkle with Parmesan cheese.

14. Spray 15-inch piece of foil with cooking spray.

15. Cover lasagna with foil.

16. Bake for 45 minutes at 350 degrees.

17. Uncover; bake 10-15 minutes longer until bubbling and/or beginning to brown.

Let stand 10 minutes before serving. Serves 8-10.

Tater Tot Casserole
– Linda K. Jitmoud

This dish is easy and great for busy mothers. Kids love it.

Ingredients

1 lb. ground beef

1 can cream of mushroom soup (organic preferable when available)

1 package, frozen tater tots

Salt and pepper to taste

⅛ cup grated cheese

Method

1. Brown the ground beef. When it's done, drain off the grease and put the ground beef in the bottom of a casserole dish.
2. Season to taste.
3. Place frozen tater tots on top of the ground beef.
4. Pour cream of mushroom soup evenly on top.
5. Mix in ½ can of milk and pour that in also.
6. Cover casserole dish and place in preheated oven at 375 degrees for 45 minutes.
7. Remove casserole dish and sprinkle grated cheese on top.
8. Continue cooking until cheese is thoroughly melted (10-15 minutes).

Quiche

– Mahasin D. Shamsid-Deen

Ingredients

5 whole eggs – large

1 cup of mayonnaise, separated into 2 halves

¼ cup milk or cream

2 tbsp. of chopped scallions

½ cup chopped meat – turkey ham or turkey bacon, chicken, or salmon

½ cup fresh chopped spinach – if frozen drain thoroughly and fluff

½ cup mild cheddar cheese - shredded

¼ cup pepper jack cheese or use a Swiss cheese and add tablespoon of chopped jalapenos

1 tsp. of Salt

½ tsp. of Pepper

½ tsp. of Paprika

1 tbsp. of chopped parsley or dried parsley

2 ripe plump tomatoes

1 large clove of garlic

9-inch deep-dish piecrust

Method

Step 1: Preheat oven to 350°

Step 2: Crush garlic clove very fine retaining juice. Add this mixture to ½ cup of mayonnaise and blend well. Cover and let set in refrigerator for at least ½ hour. (*If making homemade mayonnaise, add the garlic in right after slowly adding in the oil while blending*)

Step 3:
1. Beat the eggs.
2. Put about 2 tbsp. of this mixture into a separate bowl and set aside.
3. Add ½ cup mayonnaise and milk with a fork or whisk to rest of eggs and beat until foamy.
4. Fold in scallions, meat and spinach. Mix well.
5. Add cheeses, salt, pepper, paprika and mix well.
6. Take the small portion of beaten eggs you have set aside and give bottom and sides of crust an egg wash.

7. Pour egg and meat mixture into the piecrust. Mixture should be thick.

8. Bake in preheated oven for 1 hour. Test center of quiche to make sure egg mixture is solid. If not, continue in increments of about 7 minutes. If necessary, take aluminium foil and cover edge of the crust so it does not burn while center is still cooking.

9. While Quiche is baking, slice fresh tomatoes.

10. Add the refrigerated garlic/mayonnaise mixture on top of tomatoes.

11. Sprinkle with parsley.

12. Take cooked Quiche out of oven. Set aside to cool.

Serve Quiche with tomato slices on the side.

Note - Can substitute any green vegetable for the spinach – broccoli, sprouts, etc.

The Prophet said, "If somebody eats something forgetfully while he is fasting, then he should complete his fast, for Allah has made him eat and drink." (Hadith by Bukhari, Volume 8, Book 78, Number 662)

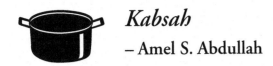

Kabsah
– Amel S. Abdullah

Ingredients

1 chicken, cut into pieces

1 onion, cut into 4 pieces

1 head of garlic, cut into chunks

2 chili peppers, cut into chunks, stems removed

1 big piece of fresh ginger, cut into chunks

6 dried lemons, also called loomi (do NOT use fresh lemons)

6-10 cinnamon sticks

15-20 whole cardamom pods

1 tsp. salt

1 tsp. black pepper

2 tsp. allspice or all-purpose Middle Eastern spice mixture

1 tsp. ground cumin

1 tsp. ground red pepper

1 tsp. ground cinnamon

1 tsp. ground ginger

½ tsp. ground turmeric

1 small package tomato paste

8 cups water

4 cups Basmati rice

Pine nuts

Yellow raisins

Finely chopped parsley

¼ stick of butter

Vegetable oil

Method

1. In a large non-stick pot coated with vegetable oil, brown the chicken pieces on medium-high heat along with the onions, garlic, chili peppers, fresh ginger, dried lemons, cinnamon sticks, and cardamom pods. Stir frequently to ensure browning on all sides.

2. While browning the chicken, sprinkle the salt and other ground spices evenly over the contents of the pot. Continue stirring at regular intervals.

3. When the chicken is nicely browned, pour the water into the pot and bring to a boil.

4. Add tomato paste to the pot, stir, and reduce the flame until the water is simmering.

5. Cover the pot and allow the chicken to simmer for 30-40 minutes.

6. Then turn off the flame.

7. Remove the chicken pieces and brown them in a separate skillet coated with vegetable oil until the skin becomes dark red (crispy but not dry or burnt).

8. Strain the broth and set aside.

9. In a large, non-stick pot coated with a modest amount of vegetable oil, stir the rice and raisins on medium-high heat until all the rice is coated with oil.

10. Add the chicken broth to the pot and bring to a boil. Stir the rice one time only to help separate the grains.

11. Immediately cover the pot and reduce the heat to low. Cook until the rice is done, usually about 20 minutes. Add more water if necessary.

12. Pour the rice out into a platter and arrange the chicken pieces on top.

13. Garnish with pine nuts toasted in butter and finely chopped parsley.

14. Serve with salad and bowls of plain yoghurt.

Tasty Mixed Vegetable Stew
– Balqees Mohammed

Ingredients

½ - 1 lb. meat with bones: your choice: beef, lamb or chicken

1 medium or large red onion, finely chopped

5 – 6 sections of garlic, finely chopped

2 tbsp. cooking oil

½ cup green beans, finely chopped into bite-sized sections

2-4 large carrots, peeled & quartered lengthwise, chopped into bite-sized pieces

3 medium potatoes, peeled & quartered lengthwise, chopped into bite-sized pieces

4 medium zucchini squash, peeled & quartered lengthwise, chopped into bite-sized pieces

½ or ¼ head of cauliflower, cleaned and chopped into bite-sized pieces

2 medium or large eggplants, cleaned (not peeled), quartered lengthwise, and chopped into bite-sized pieces

4-5 medium or large very red, ripe tomatoes, cleaned and chopped into small pieces or run through the blender

2 tbsp. tomato paste

Salt & pepper to taste

1 (or more, according to personal preference) hot chilli pepper/s

2 tsp. cumin powder

2 tsp. cinnamon powder (or 2-3 pieces cinnamon bark)

1-2 tsp. chili powder

Water (at least 2 quarts, perhaps more)

Method

1. The meat chosen for this dish should be as lean as possible. For the best flavor and nicest texture of a thick stew, meat with some bones is preferred.

2. Remove excessive fat or skin and dice to squares about ½ inch, and then set-aside until you finish preparing the vegetables.

3. Finely chop the onion and garlic and place into a large/deep saucepan.

4. Add the cooking oil, but do not sauté until you finish preparing the remainder of the vegetables.

5. Wash and drain the green beans and then cut or snip off the ends.

6. Cut the beans into fine chunks.

7. Wash and drain the carrots then peel, cut off the ends and then quarter lengthwise and chop into fine pieces.

8. Prepare the tomatoes by either finely chopping them or using an electric blender.

9. Begin the sauté process by heating the onion/garlic/oil mixture in the deep saucepan. Stir occasionally.

10. When the onions and garlic begin to brown slightly, or turn golden, add the meat and continue to stir with the onion/garlic mixture, until the meat changes color and begins to brown.

11. Add the remaining spices.

12. Add the tomatoes and tomato paste. Stir this consistently while fire still on, and let simmer slightly (about 5 minutes), until the mixture begins to lose its moisture.

13. Add the water (1-2 quarts), stirring to mix the water well with the sauté mixture.

14. Cover and let boil for about 20 minutes or more, frequently checking and stirring, to try to prevent sticking of meat and vegetables to the bottom of the pan.

15. Once the meat has cooked until well done, add the remaining vegetables to the mixture, stir well, and let the mixture continue to boil on a medium to high heat until the remaining vegetables become well done also.

16. Check the pot often, to make sure that sticking is not occurring, and if the mixture becomes too thick or dry, add some more water.

Note - This is an excellent dish for cold weather and hot alike, nice served along with a rice pilaf or salad and bread for dipping.

Potuna Casserole
– Sabah Negash

Ingredients

8 small-medium russet potatoes

1 ½ cup chopped onions

1 cup chopped mixed colored bell peppers

1 can chuck tuna [12 oz.] (In water)

1 cup shredded mild cheddar cheese

2 tbsp. cooking oil

½ tsp. salt

2 tsp. garlic & pepper seasoning

Method

1. Preheat oven to 375 degrees.
2. Clean, peel, and quarter the potatoes. Put them in a pot of water and boil until you can easily stick a fork through them.
3. Put 2 tbsp. of oil in medium size frying pan and heat. Add white onions to the pan and sauté until slightly tender.
4. Open and drain the tuna. Add tuna to the sautéed onions. Stir-fry until tuna is no longer pink.
5. Add bell peppers and continue to sauté.
6. Add your seasoning to the tuna mixture. Put aside.
7. Pour water off your potatoes. Mash the potatoes.
8. Add your tuna mixture to the mashed potatoes. Mix well.
9. Transfer the potuna into a deep-dish pan. Sprinkle with cheese.
10. Place in the oven and bake until cheese melts.

Comments - I use a brand of garlic & pepper seasoning called 'Spice Grocers.' If you can't find this brand, the important ingredients in this seasoning are: salt, pepper, garlic, marjoram, and thyme. If your brand has these ingredients, you should be fine.

Garden Puree
– Soumy Ana

Ingredients

2 large potatoes boiled and peeled

2 cups cauliflower boiled

1 cup broccoli boiled only 3 minutes

1 cup carrots boiled

¼ cup grated cheese or Parmesan

1½ cups milk

1 tbsp. butter

½ tbsp. cumin

½ tsp. salt

½ tsp. oregano

Method

1. Mash all vegetables in a mixer.
2. Put them in an oven dish.
3. Add the remaining ingredients (the milk, the spices and the cheese). Mix well.
4. Put in the oven for 15 minutes or just before serving.

Time: ½ hour
Makes: 4-8 servings.

Note - I made up this recipe one day when I wanted my children to eat more vegetables. It worked!

No Tomatoes Pizza
– Soumy Ana

Ingredients

Dough

1 cup of water

1 tbsp. olive oil

1 egg

3½ cups flour

1 tsp. yeast

Filling

Mustard

¼ cup olive oil

2 tbsp. oregano (fresh if possible) and/or basil (fresh)

1 tsp. cumin

½ tsp. salt

1 can of tuna fish

2 tbsp. Parmesan cheese

1 green pepper broiled in the oven, peeled and sliced (optional)

Mushrooms (optional)

Cooked broccoli (optional)

Method

1. Put all the dough ingredients in one container (I use a bread machine to knead the dough) and knead until you obtain a flexible smooth consistency. The dough should be elastic and should not stick to your container. Cover with plastic and let it rise, then spread the dough thinly on an oven tray or pizza stone.
2. Meantime, mix the oil with the spices and herbs.
3. Spread the mustard thinly over the dough.
4. Spread the oil-herbs-spices mixture thinly over the dough.
5. Crumble and spread the tuna over the dough as well as the vegetables. Add the Parmesan.
6. Bake in the oven at 400-450 F for about 10 minutes.

Time: 1 hour makes 8 servings.

Note - I made up this recipe one day I did not have any tomato sauce and we had a craving for pizza. Enjoy!

Kimbap (Korean sushi)
– Soumy Ana

Ingredients

4 roasted laver kelp (seaweed)

1 cup grated carrots

1 bell pepper cut in small slices or 1 cup spinach

2 whipped eggs

1 cup rice

1 tbsp. sesame oil

1 tbsp. sesame seeds roasted on a pan for a few minutes until brown.

½ tsp. cumin

4½ tsp. salt

3½ tsp. pepper

½ tsp. curry or hot pepper

Method

1. Cook the rice. When cooked, add the sesame seeds and sesame oil, salt and pepper. Mix well. You can also add soya sauce if you like it.

2. Fry the peppers with olive oil and add cumin and salt. Put aside.

3. Cook the eggs only on one side as if making an omelette. Remove as soon as the egg is cooked. Add salt and pepper. Cut the omelette in four pieces.

4. Fry the carrots for one or two minutes. Add the curry or hot pepper and some salt.

5. Get a mat (for beginners). Put the kelp on it. Put a hipping tablespoon of rice over the kelp. Flatten the rice until it sticks together in one mass. Put a piece of omelette on top. Add a tablespoon of carrots. Finally, add some fried pepper or spinach.

6. Roll everything, starting from the side closest to you. Roll everything very tightly as if rolling a carpet. When you are done rolling, the kimbap should look like a tube that stays together easily. Cut the cylinder into five.

Making time: ½ hour.
Makes: 4 servings.

Note - Kimbap [say: keemb'p] is a traditional Korean sushi. I got this recipe from a Korean friend who used to make it for me very often until she taught me how to do it myself.

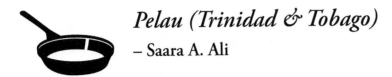

Pelau (Trinidad & Tobago)

– Saara A. Ali

Ingredients

1 tsp. salt

½ tsp. black pepper

2 tbsp. minced green onions

3 cloves garlic, minced

1 tsp. soya sauce

3 lbs. chicken, cut into pieces

2 tsp. vegetable oil

1½ tbsp. brown sugar

½ cup finely chopped onion

2 large tomatoes, chopped

2 tbsp. chopped celery

2 pimento sweet peppers, chopped finely

1 tbsp. chopped fresh thyme

1 can (14 oz.) pigeon peas

2 cups rice

1 tsp. salt

1½ cups coconut milk

3 cups water

Method

1. Combine salt, black pepper, minced green onions, minced garlic, and soya sauce and rub onto chicken. Let marinate for about 1 hour.

2. Heat oil in a large skillet. Sprinkle sugar over oil and leave it (do not stir) until it has caramelized to an almost dark brown color. The sugar may bubble up a bit.

3. Add chicken pieces and stir to ensure that they brown evenly. Stir and brown for about 3 minutes.

4. Add rice and stir well. Cook for 3 minutes more, stirring often.

5. Add onion, tomatoes, celery, pimento sweet peppers, thyme and peas. Stir to combine and cook for 5 minutes.

6. Add the salt, coconut milk and water. Stir well.

7. Bring to the boil. Lower the heat to almost low; cover and simmer until rice is cooked about 25-30 minutes. If rice is not cooked through, add hot water and continue cooking.

Definition - Sweet pimento is a variety of pepper with a slight heat that is similar to bell peppers. Pigeon peas are oval shaped peas that have a nutty flavor. Coconut Milk can be found in most large grocery stores in packets or tins. *Pelau* is a hearty one-pot rice and meat dish.

Lasagna

– Anisa Abeytia

This popular and easy to prepare dish is a great way to introduce leafy greens like collards, Swiss chard and kale into your diet. These vitamin packed greens are often times neglected because no one knows how to cook them, or do not like the taste. I have also replaced the white pasta noodles for a healthy brown rice noodle. White pasta, like white rice is an anti-nutrient food because it actually brings no nutritional value and robs the body of life giving enzymes. White pasta and rice are also an inflammatory substance and high on the glycemic index. People with inflammatory conditions should avoid white rice, white flour (and everything made with it) and of course white sugar.

Ingredients

1 Package Lasagna Brown Rice Noodles

2 cups full-fat, small curd cottage cheese

1 bunch kale, collards and Swiss chard (remove their hard spine and toss out), chopped into strips

4-5 cups of pasta sauce

1-2 bags full fat Italian cheese

1 onion, sliced

1 tablespoon each of dry oregano, basil and thyme, kelp flakes (this will not make it taste "fishy")

1-2 tablespoons coconut oil for sautéing

Sea salt

Method

1. Place the cottage cheese, spices, pinch of salt and kelp flakes into a bowl and stir until mixed well. Set aside.

2. Heat a pan for sautéing the onions.

3. After the pan is hot add in the coconut oil and the onions. Sautee for 15-20 minutes or until caramelized. Be careful to not burn the oil or it is rancid.

4. Set the pot of water for the noodles to boil.

5. After 15 minutes add in the collard, kale and chard into the onions.

6. Pour in 1-tablespoon water and cover for 5 minutes. The flame should be low.

7. Add in 1-teaspoon butter or coconut oil to the boiling water before you add in the noodles. Be careful not to over cook the noodles or they will not be workable.

8. Stir them and make sure that they stay separate and remove after 7 minutes or while still al dente. ⇨

---

9. Once the noodles are done, drain and separate the noodles and prepare to layer them into the lasagna dish.

10. Preheat the oven to 245 degrees C (475 degrees F).

Layering the Lasagna

1. Pour enough pasta sauce into the bottom of the lasagna dish to just cover it lightly.

2. Add in the first layer of noodles.

3. Pour enough pasta sauce onto them, just to cover them, like a light film.

4. Add a generous helping of the herbed cottage cheese and spread.

5. Sprinkle a handful, or to your liking, of Italian cheese over the cottage cheese.

6. Next add in a layer of the leafy greens.

7. Top the greens with a layer of pasta sauce.

8. Now add a layer of Italian cheese.

9. Add one more layer of pasta sauce.

10. Place a layer of the lasagna noodles on top of that and repeat steps 1-9. After step 9, add a layer of sauce, very thin and sprinkle some cheese.

11. Cover with a piece of unbleached parchment and then place a sheet of aluminum foil on top.

12. Place in the oven. Check it after one hour. Lift up the foil and if the pasta sauce is bubbling up, remove the parchment and foil and let the top brown, but not too much or it becomes difficult to cut.

13. Remove from the oven and let cool 30-40 minutes.

Maklubah

– Anisa Abeytia

The most popular versions of this dish are from Syria and Palestine. This recipe is mostly Palestinian. Why this recipe needs a makeover is that it is over cooked and prepared in an aluminum pan. The combination of over cooked meat, white rice and vegetables results in a food devoid of any nutrients, it is also enzymatically dead and very difficult to digest. In Morocco, honey (which is rich in enzymes) is added at the end of cooking a tajeen for digestibility. During Ramadan, digestion is already challenged. Add in a dish like this and most people will be under digestive distress. Then there is the aluminum pan that will leech Alzheimer's-causing aluminum into the food. Use a stainless steel pan instead. Non-stick and Teflon pans are equally as dangerous. Lastly, olive oil is used to braise the meat and as a result becomes carcinogenic (cancer causing).

Ingredients

- 2 cups brown rice, soaked in salted water for 2 hours and drained
- 2 lbs. or ½ kilo lamb or beef cut into cubes (you can also use a whole chicken cut into pieces)
- 2 cups onion, sliced into strips
- 1 large cauliflower (cut into flowerets), make sure that the vegetables are not cut too thick, they will not cook enough, since this recipe has them on top, away from the meat.
- 4 carrots, peeled and sliced
- 3 large potatoes, peeled and cut into chucks
- 3 large tomatoes, sliced into rounds
- 3 cups water

- 4 cloves garlic, crushed
- 4 tbsp. butter (you never fry or sauté with olive oil)
- 4-6 whole peppercorns
- 1 ½ tsp. ground cumin
- ¾ tsp. ground allspice
- ½ tsp. ground nutmeg and 4 strands of saffron
- 3 cups chicken stock

For the garnish on top

- ¼ cup blanched almonds, halved
- ¼ cup whole pine nuts
- 1 ½ tbsp. butter for frying

Method

1. Heat the stainless steel pot you will be using and add the butter.
2. When it melts add the onions and cook for 10 minutes on medium heat.
3. Add in the lamb or beef and add a pinch of salt. ⇨

---

4. Braise the meat until it is browned on both sides, on a medium heat. This step is important because it will determine the texture of the meat. If the time is too long, the meat will be tough and the same if it is not cooked long enough. This can take up to 30 minutes. You are not trying to cook the meat all the way. This is why the heat should be medium low.

5. Add in the saffron, cumin and a pinch of salt.

6. Cover with the 3 cups water and bring to a boil.

7. Reduce heat and let simmer uncovered for 20 minutes.

8. Skim the top of the water.

9. Remove from heat and using a slotted spoon, remove meat.

Layering

1. In another stainless steel pot, line the bottom with the slices of tomato.

2. Next then add the lamb and onion.

3. Crush the garlic on top of the meat.

4. Add in the spices.

5. Then add the drained rice.

6. Pour the lamb broth over everything and bring to a boil for 20 minutes.

7. Add a layer of the cauliflower, potatoes and carrots. This will help with the over cooking issue.

8. Cover and reduce the heat to medium low for 30-40 minutes cook until the water is mostly absorbed. Cook on low for 10-20 minutes, then let steam for 20-40 minutes. Make sure that there is enough water as you cook it. The rice, even when done, should not be dry, but a little moist.

Garnish Method

1. In a frying pan add the butter and let melt.

2. Add in the nuts and fry until golden. They will continue to darken after they are removed from the heat, so do not over-cook.

3. Place to the side in a bowl.

4. Place a large platter over the pot (this may require more than one person).

5. Flip the pot over while holding the plate in place. Using a spoon, loosen the rice a bit and garnish with the nuts.

Lamb Leban

Ingredients

2-3 lbs. of lamb, cut into stew sized chunks (I prefer leg with bone in, but your choice)

2 cups of leban <buttermilk> (the slightly heavier leban sold at Arabic stores works best)

- water – enough for cooking the meat
- equal amounts of both: Corn Starch and Olive oil
- Salt and pepper to taste
- Other spices to your taste, if needed

Method

1. Place seasoned meat in water, adding a little olive oil for flavor, and bring to boil.
2. After about 5 minutes turn heat down to a low boil/almost a simmer (this helps keep the lamb tender).
3. Skim water to get excess fat and blood (you know, when it forms that yucky brown thick stuff at the top). Also check if you need to add water. You want about the same amount of water as leban (buttermilk), or even a little less. More water = stronger taste.
4. When lamb is almost done, put the leban in a blender to liquefy, adding 1-2 tbsp. of cornstarch (this helps hold it together some) and just a touch of olive oil, not too much.
5. Place in a saucepan on low heat while constantly stirring until heated through. Remember that leban is dairy and dairy sticks and burns if you're not careful.
6. Once heated, add to meat and bring to a boil again, constantly stirring.
7. When it reaches a boil, turn down heat and cover. Let simmer for a few minutes (approximately 5 minutes).
8. Best served with basmati rice, vermicelli and toasted pine nuts (or almonds).

Chicken Curry with Tomatoes (Murgha Kari)

This dish from the Punjab takes only 30 minutes to prepare.
In India fresh tomatoes would be used in this dish.

Ingredients

4 medium onions, chopped

2 tbsp. curry powder

½ cup butter or cooking oil

1 cup or 1 can (8 ounces) tomato sauce

2 tsp. salt

1 frying chicken (2 to 3 pounds)

¾ cup hot water

Method

1. Use a casserole or large skillet with lid. Cook onions and curry powder in butter for 10 to 15 minutes.

2. Add tomato sauce and salt.

3. Disjoint and skin chicken, and place in sauce.

4. Cook, uncovered, over medium heat, turning frequently until sauce becomes quite dry and chicken tests done with fork, about 15 minutes.

5. Add hot water, cover pot, and cook over low heat for 5 minutes.

Makes 4 servings

Nur's Peanut Chicken Breast

Ingredients

¼ cup peanut butter

2 tbsp. chopped peanuts

2 tbsp. soy sauce

1 tbsp. minced onions

1 tbsp. minced parsley

1 clove garlic – crushed

Several drops of red pepper sauce

1/8 tsp. ground ginger

4 whole chicken breasts – skinned & boned

2 tbsp. soy sauce

2 tbsp. honey

1 tbsp. melted butter

1-⅔ cups chicken broth

1 tbsp. cornstarch

Method

1. Mix peanut butter, peanuts, 2 tbsp. soy sauce, onion, parsley, garlic, pepper sauce, and ginger. Spread on inside of each chicken breast.
2. Fold in half; close with small skewer or a toothpick.
3. Place in slow-cooking pot.
4. Mix remaining 2 tbsp. soy sauce with honey, butter, and broth; pour over chicken.
5. Cover and cook on low for 4 to 5 hours.
6. Remove chicken from pot.
7. Turn control to high.
8. Dissolve cornstarch in small amount of cold water; stir into sauce.
9. Cook on high for about 15 minutes.
10. Spoon sauce on chicken and serve.

Rose Chicken
– Norma Kassim

Ingredients

1 whole chicken – small

4 potatoes

2 large red onions

5 fresh red chillies (remove the seeds) or 1 tablespoon of chilli paste

3 stalks of lemon grass or ½ teaspoon of the powder

1 tsp. of powdered cumin (jintan putih)

½ tsp. of powdered fennel (jintan manis)

5 mint leaves

1 cup of tomato puree

½ cup of evaporated milk

½ cup of coconut milk

1 cup of cooking oil

1 tbsp. sugar

1 tbsp. salt

Method

1. Clean and cut the chicken into eight pieces.

2. Peel and cut the potatoes into 4 pieces each.

3. Grind the onions and chillies.

4. Pound lightly the lemon grass.

5. Mix the onions, chillies, cumin, fennel, lemon grass, tomato puree, evaporated milk, coconut milk, sugar and salt. Then marinade the chicken in the mixture and leave aside for ten minutes.

6. Heat the cooking oil in a Wok.

7. Gradually fry the chicken piece by piece and fry until half cooked.

8. Then pour the remainder of the sauce mixture into the Wok with the potatoes.

9. Continue to stir.

10. When the chicken and potatoes are nearly cooked, lower the fire to the minimum and leave it to boil slowly.

11. Add the mint leaves and stir well.

Serve the chicken with boiled, white rice.

Green Chile and Chicken Enchiladas

– Linda D. Delgado

Ingredients

1 whole chicken

24 corn tortillas

1 can cream of chicken soup

1 can cream of mushroom soup

1 medium onion, finely chopped

1 pound of longhorn natural cheese, grated

Olive Oil for coating corn tortillas (approximately 1 cup needed)

2 cans of chopped green chile or 12 fresh green chiles finely chopped

1-2 cups of chicken stock

Method

1. Boil the chicken until tender, remove from pot and cool, remove skin, debone and separate into bite size pieces.

2. Place chicken soup and mushroom soup in a large cooking pot.

3. Add the chopped onion and chile. Add chicken pieces. Add chicken stock.

3. Heat until this mixture is warm. Pour olive oil in a skillet. Heat to warm temperature.

4. In a deep baking dish cover the bottom of the dish with the chicken mixture.

5. Then using tongs cover a corn tortilla in the warm olive oil and then place it on the chicken mixture.

6. Continue this procedure until the first layer covers the mixture.

7. Spoon the chicken mixture over the layer of corn tortillas.

8. Sprinkle grated cheese over the first layer of chicken mixture and corn tortillas.

9. Continue layering chicken mixture, tortillas and cheese until all corn tortillas are used.

10. Cover baking dish with aluminum foil and bake at 325 degrees for 30-45 minutes or until corn tortillas are soft and moist.

Curry Anything with Whatever
– Nancy E. Biddle

This recipe includes how to make a basic curry and then provides different options for preparing a curry with various kinds of vegetables, meats, and fish. The author has included a number of helpful cooking tips in the methods sections, which may be helpful to the novice for making curry.

From the author: "I married a South Asian man and had to quickly learn how to master the South Asian dish "Curry". I am going to provide a few basics about making a successful Curry in the easiest way possible, and as a side tip, how to make a biryani."

Required Cooking Appliances

A pressure cooker

A food processor

A hand Mixer

A top from another pot that more or less fits the width of the pressure cooker.

Recommended Ingredients

The ingredients listed below should be on hand to make a Curry Sauce with Anything (meat, fish or vegetable). The type of meat to be cooked with the curry sauce will determine which ingredients you use.

Ground Turmeric

Ground Coriander Seed

Ground Red Chilli

Dried Rubbed Methi leaves

Ground Cumin

Garam Masala (mixture of spices common to Indian dishes)

Cooking oil (Corn or Olive)

Ghee (not vegetable based; Ghee is clarified butter)

Dried Apricots

Cinnamon Bark

Cloves

Black and Green Cardamom

Red Tomatoes (baseball sized, or Romano)

Green Bell Peppers (hand sized)

Onions (Red or Yellow)

Garlic

Ginger "finger" (middle finger long, two fingers wide)

Step One - Ingredients for a Curry Sauce Base

2 (two) round tomatoes or four Romano sized tomatoes.

1 Green Pepper

1 ginger finger

Method for Base

1. Peel the garlic and the ginger, chop into a few pieces and put in the food processor.

2. Whizz this up first. The ginger is hard so you want to break it down first.

3. Peel and chop the onion into a few pieces and add to the garlic-ginger mixture, whizz a bit.

4. Wash and cut out the tomato stem base and chop a few times and add to the processor.

5. Wash and seed the green pepper, chop and add to the processor and whizz up the lot until well blended.

Method Note 1: This can be played around with for more bitter or sweeter results. For example, add another tomato for a sweeter curry, or add a ½ green pepper for a more bitter curry. Add a thumb-sized bit of ginger for a sharper taste; add another ball of garlic for a more peppery bite. Note that onion, ginger and garlic add a "hot" sensation. The more you use in the base, the spicier the result. If you need a bit more sauce, add an onion.

Method Note 2: This is your sauce base. You can cook this up with the spices and oil (see below for proportions) alone and reserve for a later use.

Method Note 3: In this base you can make *Curry Anything with Whatever*.

Anything Ideas: for meat and poultry with bone, fish or vegetables.

Meat Ingredient Options

Lamb (with bone) 2 lbs. butcher-cut into pieces

Goat (with bone) 2 lbs. butcher-cut into pieces

Beef (with bone) 2 lbs. butcher-cut into pieces

Ground Beef (Keema) (lean!) 1-2 lbs.

Chicken (Legs are juicier, more flavourful and more nutritious than breast) 5-6 legs butcher-cut into two pieces each. ⇨

Fish Ingredient Options

White Fish (white is best, I personally do not think salmon or trout blends well in a curry, best bet for fish is a Bengali food market)

Shrimp etc. If selecting fish you would need to prepare the sauce ahead.

Vegetable Ingredient Options

Roots like carrot, turnip, potato, and parsnip

Flowers like broccoli, cauliflower

Greens like spinach, mustard leaf, Italian broccoli, and kale

Pulse (legumes), like green peas, green beans, chickpeas, etc. (dried or canned)

Method Note 4: When cooking a "meat" based curry, the Vegetables and Pulses options can be the "Whatever". For example: Chicken Chana (Chicken with mashed split chick peas), Keema aloo mater (Ground beef with potato and peas) Lamb Gobi (with Cauliflower).

Cooking Stage Part 1: Making it Edible

Get out the pressure cooker and put it on the stovetop.

Give the meat or chicken a rinse and drain. If frozen defrost completely in running cool water. If meat is still icy it will come out tough.

Pour the curry base mixture into the pot. Swish the food processor with a cup or so of water and reserve.

Add the spices as follows:

⅓ tbsp. Turmeric (this spice is bitter, and also thickens the sauce)

1 rounded tbsp. Coriander

1 scant tbsp. or 2 level tsp. red chilli powder (to taste: use less if you need mild, use more if you need spicy)

1 tbsp. salt (this can be adjusted later)

Add the meat and stir.

Judge the liquid and add between 1-3 cups of water as needed. You want to cover the meat, meaning the water reaches the level of the top most pieces of meat and a little more.

Method Note 5:

If making chicken curry, add just a cup or none at all. Chicken produces its own water.

If making just sauce add 1-2 cups of water.

If cooking root vegetables use a ratio of 2:1, two cups of vegetable, 1 cup of water.

Fix the pressure cooker lid as per manufacturer instructions and let the pressure rise. Once hissing cook for the following times:

For Lamb and Goat: Cook for 35 minutes

For Beef: Cook for 40 minutes

For Chicken or Ground meat: Cook for 25 minutes. (Chicken can also be cooked without pressure for 35 minutes with occasional stirring and a good fitting lid.)

For root vegetables: Cook for 10-15 minutes

For Flowers: Cook for 5-10 minutes

For dried whole chick peas (After soaking for 2-3 hours and rubbed so the skin is removed): 45 minutes

For canned chickpeas (rinse and rub the skins off): 15-20 minutes.

For split dried chickpeas (already skinned, pre-soak for 2-3 hours): 35 minutes

For split red or yellow pulse (no need to pre-soak): Cook for 15-20 minutes.

For black pulse (pre-soak 1 hour): Cook for 20 minutes.

Cooking Stage Part 2: Browning

1. Remove from pressure cooker (As per manufacturer directions, let steam escape completely. Remember contents and pot itself are very hot)

   Note: The fastest way to cool it is to immerse the pot half way in a sink full of cold water. The pressure indicator will fall.

2. With a fork lift the pressure cap slightly to release any left over steam. Remove the lid opening it away from your face. Dry off the bottom of the pot and return to the stove.

3. Check the contents to make sure the "anything" is "cooked".

   Note: Cooked means the meat or chicken separates easily from the bone.

4. Check the sauce for salt and add more if needed.

   Note: If the red meat pieces are still tough pressure cook for another ten minutes or so. ⇨

5. Add about a cup of oil or ghee to the pot and stir.

6. Bring to a boil and cover with a loose lid and simmer on medium for about ten minutes until the oil separates.

   Note: If you want to make a quick briyani to the meat or chicken curry, add 5-10 black cardamons, 2-3 cinnamon bark and 3-4 whole cloves at this browning point.

Adjusting Stage Part 3: Adding the Whatever, Reducing, and Final Taste Touches

For meat or chicken curries, if you are adding a Whatever, add it now, and continue boiling with the lid partially off. Use your judgement about liquid, it may need a cup or two more water while the Whatever cooks but as the mixture boils further it will reduce.

Method Note 6: The Whatever you chose is a compliment to the meat, or the meat is a compliment to the Whatever, depending on the amount of Whatever you are adding. Be careful of the balance. For example, aloo-gobi gosht is mostly potato and cauliflower with some goat for flavouring. While Gosht aloo-gobi is mostly a meat curry with some potato and cauliflower pieces.

Options:

When adding potato and or cauliflower at this stage cube or cut into smaller pieces. Use one or two potatoes, and one or two heads of cauliflower.

You can rinse frozen peas to loosen them, add a ¼ tsp. of sugar to the pot if using older peas.

If adding chana (chickpeas) it must already be pre-cooked, if canned, remove the liquid and add.

For Biryani:

Add the drained rice (pre-soak the rice for 1-2 hours) and stir to distribute evenly. Eye the liquid ratio. Add enough water so that if you put your index finger into the liquid until the tip touches the surface of the rice/food the water almost covers the nail.

Put a good fitting lid on the pot and bring to a boil and let boil for ten minutes. Do not stir. Wet a clean dishtowel and wring out.

After ten minutes lift the lid; lay the towel over the top to cover the pot opening, return the lid on top of the towel, and lift any drooping corners on top.

Turn off the burner and remove the pot to a cool burner and let sit for twenty minutes. Any remaining liquid will be absorbed and the trapped steam will finish cooking the rice so it is fluffy.

For all other curries:

The final stage is reducing, but use this guide:

If serving the curry with rice, let the gravy be a bit thinner.

If serving the curry with pita or naan, let the gravy be thicker.

In the last five minutes of reducing, add a palmful of rubbed Methi leave, rub it a little more between your fingers to break it down a bit more. Methi by the way is a digestive aid.

Do not add Methi to Biryani

Remove from the heat and let cool enough to handle, transfer to a serving dish, and sprinkle on a few pinches of Cumin or Garam Masala for "looks". And serve.

Final Note

If you are in a hurry, all of the stages can be accomplished in one cooking stage: bung meat, base, spices, oil, and whatever compliments into the pressure cooker raw and bring to pressure and cook the lot for 45 minutes and presto! Just remember that the secret of South Asian food is the blending of all the flavours. Longer slow cooking produces the best result. Also, you will find, curry eaten the next day is even better.

The Holy Qur'an 5:4 They ask thee what is lawful to them (as food). Say: lawful unto you are (all) things good and pure.

Lamb Samosas from Scratch: A Family Recipe
– Amina Malik

The Story Behind the Recipe

One of the blessings of a Muslim home is the unity of family. There are many activities, spiritual and fun, that Muslim families do together. One of my cherished family memories is something quite different - cooking together as a family.

Cooking together actually happened rarely but when it came to making samosas, all of the women in the family would come together to help. This included my mum and two sisters, all working side by side to create delicious triangular treats, encased in wafer-thin pastry layers, all made by hand. Once the filling and pastry were prepared, it was a case of creating a production line with mum lightly cooking the pastry, my younger sister folding the pastry into cones, and my elder sister and I filling the cones and sealing.

Now and again I still have the privilege of taking part in this event, years after marrying and leaving the family home, and it is always fun and a time for family bonding. Because mum likes to make the pastry from scratch, several hands are needed to make the samosas, which involve various stages of preparation. These days, people buy the pastry ready-made but mum's recipe will give you the tastiest and crispiest samosas you have ever had!

Samosas are eaten the world over, and in the South Asian sub-continent fillings are traditionally either meat or vegetable. Using mum's traditional lamb samosa recipe below, you could try swapping the minced lamb for minced chicken - an unusual alternative but equally delicious. You can also make a vegetarian version using an all-vegetable filling, consisting of tiny chunks of diced potato and peas. However, here is my favorite of mum's samosa recipes – lamb and pea samosas.

Ingredients

Oil (sunflower works best)

2 lb minced lamb (called *keema* in the Asian sub-continent)

1 cup garden peas

1 onion sliced finely

2 cloves of garlic crushed

1 tsp. ground coriander

1 tsp. chilli powder

½ tsp. salt

1 tsp. chopped fresh coriander

Method for filling:

1. Coat the bottom of a pan with oil.

2. Add the *keema*, sliced onion and dry spices.

3. Stir regularly to avoid the *keema* sticking to the pan.

4. The *keema* will leave its own water in the pan. Once the water has disappeared, add 1 cup of water to cover the *keema*.

5. Place the lid on the pan and simmer for 30 minutes until cooked.

6. When there is very little water left in the pan, add the peas.

7. Check to see if the *keema* is cooked. The water in the pan should have disappeared and the onions should be completely soft. The peas should be al dente.

8. Set aside to cool whilst you prepare the pastry.

Method for pastry:

This recipe will make enough pastry for 24 samosas and you will need:

> 1 cup plain flour
>
> 2 tsp. salt
>
> 2 tbs. vegetable oil
>
> a bowl of water

1. Mix flour and salt in a bowl.

2. Make a well into the centre and add the oil and enough water to make a firm dough.

3. Knead the dough on a floured surface until smooth and roll into a ball.

4. Cover in clingfilm and set aside at room temperature for 10 minutes.

5. Divide the dough into 12 equal pieces.

6. Roll each piece into a ball and roll out into a circle of 6 in. (like a *roti* or *chapatti*) but fairly thick.

7. Use your fingertips to rub a thin layer of oil all over the *roti*.

8. Repeat the process with another ball of dough.

9. Place your second *roti* on top of the first, the two oily sides meeting.

10. Continue this process until you have 5 *rotis* stacked up.

11. Roll all of the *rotis* together until they are very thin.

12. Place the entire stack onto a warm *tawa* (a flat iron griddle pan) under medium heat, and let it cook for 20 seconds. Your aim is to firm the *roti* on one side, not to cook it, so do not leave it long enough to color.

13. Flip the entire stack so the other side cooks.

14. Using a pallet knife, remove the first *roti* from the top of the stack and put on to a plate. ⇨

15. Flip the stack again and repeat the process until all *rotis* are off the *tawa*. You should now have a stack of *rotis* that have been lightly cooked on one side each.

16. Cut these into half with a knife until you are left with a stack of semi-circles.

Putting the samosas together (get friends or family to help you!)

1. Take one semi-circle of *roti* at a time. The uncooked side should be on the outside.

2. Brush each edge with a little water and form a cone shape around your fingers, bringing the pastry further along one side so there is a flap left at the top. Seal the dampened edge by pressing with your fingers.

3. Fill the cases with your filling until it is full but leaving a quarter of an inch at the top so the remaining visible pastry acts as a flap.

4. Dab water on to the flap of pastry with your fingers and press down to seal.

5. Check for any gaps in the samosa at this stage and apply flour and water to form a paste to any cracks. Cracks in the samosa now will mean oil entering the samosa later during cooking.

6. Deep fry the samosas in hot oil until crisp and brown.

7. Leave to drain on a paper towel.

The Holy Qur'an 6:118 "So eat of (meats) on which Allah's name hath been pronounced, if ye have faith in His signs."

Side Dishes & Breads

Tuna Croquettes

– Sabah Negash

Ingredients

2 cans [12 oz.] chunk tuna (in water)

1 egg

1 cup finely chopped onions

8 saltine crackers

1 tsp. black pepper

1 tsp. seasoning salt

1 tsp. garlic powder

2 cups yellow corn meal

Method

1. Drain water off tuna. Place in large mixing bowl.
2. Mix finely chopped onions, egg and seasoning into the bowl with the tuna. Mix well.
3. Crush saltine crackers into the tuna mixture.
4. Heat some cooking oil in a frying pan on medium heat.
5. Take a large heaping spoonful of tuna mixture (two tablespoons) and make a ball.
6. Slightly flatten the ball to make a thick patty.
7. Coat the patty in the yellow corn meal.
8. Fry the patties until crispy and golden brown on both sides.

Comments - Depending on size and thickness of the croquettes, makes approximately 8-12 tuna croquettes.

Cabbage and Tuna Egg Rolls
– Sabah Negash

Ingredients

1 pkg. Coleslaw mix

1 pkg. egg roll wrappers

1 can of Tuna (12 ounce)

¼ cup water

1 tsp. salt

1 tbsp. of a blend of spices that bring out the flavor of foods

Shredded sharp cheddar cheese

Method

1. Heat tuna in large skillet on medium heat.

2. Add in coleslaw, water, salt, and seasoning.

3. Cover and steam until cabbage is tender.

4. Set mixture aside and allow it to cool completely.

5. Place a heaping spoonful of cabbage mixture and a sprinkle of cheese in center of egg roll wrapper. Follow wrapping instruction on egg roll wrapper package.

6. Fry until golden brown.

Makes approximately 20 egg rolls.

Definition - *Cream of Wheat* is made of farina, a fine grain similar to semolina that is popularly used as a breakfast cereal or porridge. Rice flour or fine semolina can be substituted for the *Cream of Wheat* in this recipe.

The Holy Qur'an 59:10 "Our Lord! Forgive us our sins as well as those of our brethren who preceded us in faith and let not our hearts entertain any unworthy thoughts or feelings against [any of] those who have believed. Our Lord! You are indeed full of kindness and Most Merciful."

Brown Rice

– Anisa Abeytia

All over Asia, rice is a staple food whose importance cannot be overstated. Many nutritional deficiencies occur when white rice is consumed, the most notable is a thiamine (B1) deficiency, which can result in Beri Beri or a niacin (B3) deficiency, also known as Pellagra (Fallon, Sally, *Nourishing Traditions*, 38). The B vitamins are essential to maintain health, and B3 is important in maintaining heart health. Interestingly, both Beri Beri and Pellagra were unknown conditions before the introduction of white rice. Both these conditions are not disease, but the result of nutrient deficiency. If you throw in some dry fruit and nuts, no one will know the difference.

Ingredients

4 cups brown rice

6 cups water

1 strip Kombu (edible kelp)

2 tbsp. butter

½ diced onion

4 garlic cloves, minced

1 pinch saffron

1 tsp. turmeric

Salt

Method

1. In a stockpot, heat butter and add in onions. Fry for 1-2 minutes.

2. Add in garlic and fry for 1-2 minutes.

3. Pour in the water and add in the Kombu and enough salt to taste.

4. Bring to a boil.

5. Add in turmeric and saffron and rice.

6. Cover (leave a space for the steam to escape) and let boil for 15-20 minutes. Keep an eye on it and add water as needed.

7. Reduce heat to medium and let cook for 15 minutes.

8. Reduce heat to a simmer and let cook for another 15 minutes.

9. Remove from heat and let sit until absolutely tender.

Sage Sausage

– Anisa Abeytia

Ingredients

2-3 lbs. ground chicken

2 tbsp. dry sage

1 tbsp. dried thyme

1 large piece of an onion

1-2 tbsp. coconut oil

Salt

Method

1. In a frying pan heat the oil.
2. Add in onion and sauté for 10 minutes to infuse the oil with its flavor.
3. Remove the onion from the oil.
4. In a large bowl, place chicken and herbs in the bowl and pour the oil in. Mix well.
5. Roll one into ball, flatten and fry one in the same pan to check flavor.
6. Once you reach the flavor that you like, divide the mixture in two.
7. Roll one of the balls out into a log and wrap in parchment.
8. Wrap the parchment in two layers of plastic wrap and place in the freezer.
9. When you would like to use it, pull it out, and remove the plastic.
10. Slice into rounds with a sharp knife.
11. The other batches, roll into balls, flatten and fry in coconut oil.

Potato Kebabs
– Pakistan

Ingredients

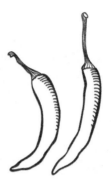

5 lbs. Potatoes (Red, medium sized)

1 cup chopped Green Chilies

1 bunch of chopped Cilantro

1 tbsp. Cumin

¼ cup Pomegranate seed - dried

2 Eggs

1 tsp. Red Chili powder

1 tsp. Salt

Oil for frying

Method

1. Boil and then peel potatoes. Set aside to cool.

2. Mash potatoes (use your hands for more fun!)

3. Add -- salt, green & red chilies, pomegranate seeds, cumin, cilantro and mix well.

Crack and mix two eggs in a steel bowl.

4. Meanwhile, heat small amount of oil in frying pan.

5. Take even portions of potato mix to make 2 inch round balls then flatten to kebab shape.

6. Dip kebabs into the eggs and then fry, 5 minutes on each side.

Chorizo (Mexican Sausage)

Ingredients

1 lb. regular ground turkey, NOT ground turkey breast--some fat is necessary for the best flavor.

2 cloves garlic, crushed

1 tbsp. chili powder

1 tbsp. white vinegar

1 tsp. dried oregano

Method

1. Mix all the ingredients in a medium-size mixing bowl.
2. Let sit for several hours or overnight before using so flavors can blend.

Makes 1 lb.

Note - ¼ cup of this recipe equals 1 chorizo sausage in a recipe. The sausage will keep well for several days in the refrigerator, but transfer it to a glass or pottery bowl or jar. You'll never get the smell of it out of plastic!

Brown it and add to chili instead of ground beef. Cook it and eat with chutney, or fry it with eggs for some great tasting scrambles eggs. Great when served inside a flour tortilla.

Spiced Cranberry Rolls

Ingredients

1 cup milk

4 tbsp. approximately unsalted butter

¼ cup plus 2 tbsp. sugar

½ tsp. salt

2 packages (¼ ounce each) active dry yeast

¼ cup warm water (110 to 115 degrees F)

2 eggs at room temperature, lightly beaten

½ tsp. ground ginger

½ tsp. freshly grated nutmeg

4 ½ cups plus 2 tbsp. all-purpose flour

⅔ cup chopped fresh cranberries

Method

1. In a small saucepan, bring the milk to a boil over moderately high heat.

2. Remove from the heat and stir in the butter, ¼ cup of the sugar and the salt until dissolved.

3. Let cool to lukewarm.

4. In a large bowl, sprinkle the yeast over the warm water. Set aside for 5 minutes.

5. Whisk in the warm milk mixture, beaten eggs, ginger and nutmeg.

6. With a wooden spoon, stir in 4 cups of the flour until incorporated.

7. Dust a work surface with ¼ cup of the flour.

8. Turn out the dough and knead for about 6 minutes, adding about ¼ cup more flour by tablespoons to make smooth, slightly sticky dough.

9. On the work surface, sprinkle the remaining 2 tbsp. flour and 2 tbsp. sugar over the cranberries and quickly knead them into the dough. The dough will be sticky and wet.

10. Transfer the dough to a lightly greased large bowl and cover with plastic wrap.

11. Let rise in a warm place until doubled in bulk, about 40 minutes.

12. Lightly butter 2 large baking sheets.

13. Turn the dough out onto a well-floured surface and roll it out ½ inches thick.

14. With a 2½ inch biscuit cutter, cut into rounds.

15. Re-roll the scraps and cut out more rounds. Plump each round into a ball by pulling the edges under and pinching the dough at the bottom.

16 Place the rolls seam side down on the prepared baking sheets, 1 inch apart.

17. Cover with a kitchen towel and let rest for 30 minutes.

18. Preheat the oven to 350 degrees F. Set the racks in the upper and lower thirds of the oven.

19. Bake the rolls for 10 minutes, then switch the baking sheets and bake for 6 to 8 minutes longer until nicely browned.

Serve warm. Makes About 2 Dozen Rolls.

The Holy Qur'an 7:126 "Our Lord! Pour out on us patience and constancy, and make us die as those who have surrendered themselves unto You."

Apricot Wheat Bread

Ingredients

3 cups whole-wheat flour

3 tsp. baking powder

1 tsp. cinnamon

½ tsp. salt

⅛ tsp. nutmeg

1¼ cups milk

1 cup honey

1 egg, slightly beaten

2 tbsp. salad oil

1 cup diced dried apricots

1 cup walnut pieces

Method

1. In medium bowl, stir together flour, baking powder, cinnamon, salt and nutmeg.

2. Combine milk, honey, egg and oil; pour over dry ingredients.

3. Stir just enough to dampen flour.

4. Fold in apricots and walnuts.

5. Pour into a greased 9"x3" loaf pan.

6. Bake in 350-degree oven 60 to 70 minutes or until done (tooth pick comes out clean).

7. Remove from oven; let stand for about 10 minutes.

8. Remove from the pan.

9. Store overnight for easier slicing.

Hamburger or Sandwich Rolls

– Christine Amina Benlafquih

When we couldn't find proper hamburger rolls in Morocco, I learned to make my own.

Gone are the days of hamburger meals being a quick and easy meal choice, but the result is worth the effort. I've yet to serve these rolls to company without being asked for the recipe.

Ingredients

9 cups of flour

½ cup of sugar

2 tsp. salt

9 tbsp. butter, either very soft or melted

2 tbsp. wet yeast or 2 packets dry yeast

2 cups milk, very warm

1 cup water, very warm

Vegetable oil for greasing pans and brushing on rolls

Method

1. Mix the dry ingredients; add the butter, yeast and liquids. Mix to form dough, adding a little water or flour as necessary to achieve soft, sticky dough. (*) Knead until smooth either by hand or in a mixer with dough hook.

2. Place kneaded dough in a well-oiled bowl, turning once to coat the dough with oil. Cover with a heavy towel and leave to rise until doubled in bulk.

3. Turn the dough out onto your work surface (lightly flour the surface if necessary), and separate the dough into balls about the size of plums. You should have approximately 24 to 30 pieces. Roll/shape each piece of dough into smooth balls. Place on oiled baking sheets, and flatten slightly. Cover with towel and leave to rise until doubled; about an hour.

4. Preheat oven to 425 degrees. Bake 15 to 20 minutes, or until golden (not dark) brown. Remove from oven, and very lightly brush oil (or melted butter) on the tops of the rolls. Place on rack and cover with a light towel to cool. The towel holds in the steam and keeps the bread soft rather than crusty.

*Note - For a very light roll, it's best to have the dough almost too sticky to handle while kneading; this will correct itself after the dough rises.

Hint - If placing both pans in the oven at the same time, halfway through baking switch pans from top and lower racks to ensure even browning.

Asian Stuffed Peppers

Ingredients

⅔ cup uncooked curly Chinese-style noodles or angel hair pasta, broken into thirds

2 large red bell peppers

1 cup cubed firm tofu (about 6 ounces)

2 tbsp. hoisin sauce

1 tbsp. low-sodium soy sauce

2 tsp. dark sesame oil

2 garlic cloves, minced

½ cup diagonally sliced snow peas

½ cup (1½ inch) julienne-cut carrot

2 tbsp. chopped fresh cilantro

Method

1. Cook noodles according to package directions, omitting salt and fat; drain.

2. Cut each bell pepper in half lengthwise, and discard seeds and membranes. Arrange pepper halves in a 9-inch pie plate. Cover with heavy-duty plastic wrap. Microwave at high 5 minutes or until crisp-tender; drain. Return peppers to pie plate.

3. Combine tofu, hoisin sauce, and soy sauce in a small bowl; set aside.

4. Heat oil in a nonstick skillet over medium-high heat.

5. Add garlic; sauté 15 seconds.

6. Add peas and carrot; sauté 3 minutes or until vegetables are tender.

7. Add tofu mixture; sauté for 1 minute or until thoroughly heated.

8. Stir in noodles.

9. Divide noodle mixture evenly among pepper halves; sprinkle each pepper half with 1½ tsp. cilantro.

Tortilla Espanola (Spanish Potato Omelet)

Ingredients

6 cups thinly sliced peeled baking potato (about 3 pounds)

2 cups thinly sliced sweet onion

Cooking spray

2 tbsp. olive oil, divided

¾ tsp. kosher salt, divided

4 large eggs

Oregano sprigs (optional)

Method

Tortilla Espanola (its relation to Mexican tortillas comes solely from its round shape) is among the most popular dishes in Spain. Although its ingredients couldn't be more basic--potatoes, eggs, onions, and oil--they're combined and cooked in a way that makes this dish irresistible and versatile. The potatoes are normally fried, but we've roasted them with excellent results. Unlike American omelets, this one's best made several hours ahead then served at room temperature.

1. Preheat oven to 350 degrees.
2. Place the potato and onion in a roasting pan coated with cooking spray.
3. Drizzle with 1 tbsp. plus 2 tsp. oil, and sprinkle with ½ tsp. salt.
4. Toss well. Bake at 350 degrees for 1 hour or until potatoes are tender, stirring occasionally with a metal spatula to prevent sticking.
5. Combine eggs and ¼ tsp. salt in a large bowl.
6. Stir in potato mixture; let stand 10 minutes.
7. Heat 1 tsp. oil in an 8-inch nonstick skillet over medium heat.
8. Pour potato mixture into pan (pan will be very full).
9. Cook 7 minutes or until almost set, gently shaking pan frequently.
10. Place a plate upside down on top of omelet; invert onto plate. Carefully slide omelet, cooked side up, into pan; cook 3 minutes or until set, gently shaking pan occasionally.
11. Carefully loosen omelet with a spatula; gently slide omelet onto a plate.
12. Cool.
13. Cut into wedges. Garnish with oregano, if desired.

Baba Ghanouj
– Balqees Mohammed

A delicious appetizer at any meal!

Ingredients

2 medium Eggplants

Parsley (10 sprigs or so)

1 Lemon for mixture, and more for garnish

2 cloves of garlic, crushed

1 Tomato for garnish

½ cup Sesame Tahini Sauce

¼ cup Olive Oil

2 tbsp. Vinegar

Salt to taste (1-2 tsp.)

½ - 1 cup Water

Method

1. Clean and prepare eggplants. Bake in oven at 350° F for about 20 minutes, or well done. *(Note on preparation and baking at the end).

2. Remove skins from the eggplants, and place inner 'meat' of eggplants immediately in blender with the vinegar, salt and juice of one lemon. Run the blender for about one minute, until the eggplant mixture is fully mixed and all large particles are finely blended into a smooth paste texture.

3. Add the tahini sauce, olive oil and water, and run the blender once more. The final mixture should be that of a pasty substance similar to sour cream in consistency. If it is terribly runny, then add some more tahini. If it is terribly stiff, then add some more vinegar and olive oil. Do not add water – this will only make it stiffer once mixed.

4. In a mixing bowl, combine the eggplant/tahini mixture, chopped parsley and crushed garlic.

5. Serve on flat plates by spooning the mixture around the plate to cover completely, keeping the section in the center lower than the surrounding edges. (Can be served on one large plate for the table, or several smaller plates for individuals or sections of the table.)

6. Garnish with diced tomato placed intermittently around the edges or in the center, some sprigs of parsley, and about 2 tbsp. of olive oil poured into the center low spot.

7. Served with pita bread for dipping.

Note on preparing the eggplants - When baking, they tend to explode in the oven. To avoid this, poke several holes in each with a knife before placing in oven. When skinning the baked eggplants, it is helpful to hold onto the stem, cut through the stem end without completely cutting off all of the skin on opposite side, then continue to cut the inner 'meat' of the eggplant away from the skin. A fork can be helpful in this process as well. To avoid excess discoloring of the eggplant as it is removed from the skin, it is important to blend it quickly with vinegar, salt and lemon juice.

The Prophet Muhammad (peace be upon him) said: "Feed the hungry, visit the sick and set free the captives." (Sahih Al-Bukhari, Volume 7, Hadith 552.)

Samboosa

– Balqees Mohammed

Samboosa is a pastry filled with a mixture of minced meat, minced chicken, vegetables, or cheese. It is most commonly deep-fried, but can be baked in the oven if preferred. It is a popular appetizer or finger food served in many Middle Eastern regions and in the Indo-Asia area. It is a popular opening food served with coffee, juice and soup at the first meal of the evening after the breaking of the fast during the month of Ramadan in these regions.

Pastry:

3 cups flour

1 egg

1 tbsp. oil

1 tsp. salt

1 tbsp. yeast

Water – enough for mixing fine dough

2-3 cups vegetable oil for deep-frying or 2 eggs & sesame seeds for baking

Filling

One of the following:

1 lb. ground meat, or 1 lb. ground chicken, or 1 lb. white cheese, or 2 cups finely diced mixed vegetables

1 cup finely chopped parsley

¼ cup finely chopped green onions

Ingredients
Preparing the dough

1. Place all of the dry ingredients into a large mixing bowl, and stir with wooden spoon to blend, leaving an indent in the center in which to pour the liquid ingredients.

2. Add egg, oil and 1 cup of water in the beginning. Mix thoroughly with hand until the dough becomes either crumbly or starts sticking together. If the dough is still terribly crumbly, add more water to gather it together into a gum-like consistency.

3. Turn out onto a lightly floured surface, or inside the mixing bowl if large enough, and knead the dough thoroughly until it no longer sticks to your hands or the surface.

4. Set aside and cover with lid or towel, until you complete the preparation of the filling.

Preparing the filling (choose one of the following three):

1. Place the ground meat or chicken into a shallow fry pan, stirring constantly on medium to high heat until thoroughly browned and all liquid has evaporated. If you feel the meat is not done when all liquid has evaporated, you can add ½ cup water, and continue stirring until completely dry and meat begins to stick to the pan. Pour into large serving plate (to help achieve cooling), and mix in the chopped parsley and green onions. Add salt and pepper to taste.

2. Finely chop each of the vegetables you intend to use in the filling (the best choice combination for this is carrots, zucchini, green pepper, cabbage and corn). Blanch cook the carrots and zucchini in about ½ cup water in a shallow fry pan until all liquid is evaporated. Add green pepper, corn and cabbage, and stir on heat without adding any more liquid for 1-2 minutes, or until any liquid released from the heating of the vegetables is evaporated. Add salt and pepper to taste. For an added flavor, you can add one or ½ bouillon cube. However, if you do this, then go very lightly on adding any salt.

3. Place the white cheese (the best for this is a type of feta cheese which is rather soft in consistency and not crumbly-however if not available, then any feta cheese will do, or cream cheese as alternative). Mix in the green onions and parsley, and one egg, and mix all thoroughly until the cheese is completely absorbed by the egg. Do not add salt or pepper to this mixture.

Method of preparation of pastries:

1. Split the dough into four balls. Working with each ball one at a time, roll out to about ⅛ inch thickness.

2. Spoon about ½ to 1 tbsp. of filling onto the dough at a point approximately 1 inch from edge. Carefully lift edge of dough up and over filling to cover, press in crescent shaped line around the outer edges of the filling, then cut away from remainder of rolled-out dough. Keep the cut line approximately ⅛ inch away from filling so as to ensure it does not fall out when cut away.

3. Pinch around the edges of the formed pastry to ensure firm closure of the edges all around and place on a well-oiled plate until you have 7-10 pastries completed and ready for frying.

4. Fry in a pan of hot oil approximately 2 inches deep until golden brown. Turn frequently to avoid excess ballooning of pastries in hot oil.

5. Remove to paper-towel lined plate or baking dish for absorption of excess oil. Cover lightly with paper towels and place in oven to remain hot until serving. ⇨

Alternative method of cooking the pastries:

If you do not want to fry the pastries, or need to avoid fried foods, they can be baked in the oven. This method requires you to prepare all the pastries at one time rather than in bunches as in the frying method. Once each pastry has been properly formed, place it on a well-greased cookie sheet. If you need to avoid even this amount of oil, then spray the sheet with baking spray to avoid sticking to the pan after baking. With pastry brush, coat the topside of each pastry well with a mixture of egg & water. Sprinkle on browned sesame seeds and/or black caraway seeds (each optional). Bake in pre-heated oven at 350 degrees F for approximate 15-20 minutes. If the outer edges become browned before the top begins to brown, turn off the lower burner and light the upper one to brown the tops. This will not take long, so carefully watch them at this stage. Take out and let cool before removing from pan.

Makes 16-30 crescent-shaped pastries.

The Prophet said, "Nobody has ever eaten a better meal than that which one has earned by working with one's own hands. The Prophet of Allah, David used to eat from the earnings of his manual labor." (Hadith by Bukhari, Volume 3, Book 34, Number 286)

Desserts

7-UP Cake

– Mahasin D. Shamsid-Deen

This 7-UP Cake is a staple EID dish for many indigenous Muslims of the U.S. It is usually served with milk or hot un-sweetened tea. It is a form of pound cake and is the most popular with indigenous Muslims in the South-eastern part of the U.S. After attending three Eid parties with this cake and having been served it in my own home by my mother, I finally stopped just eating the cake, but learned this recipe when I was about 30 years old and it has been on my Eid table every since.

Ingredients

3 sticks of SOFTENED Butter (do not substitute)

3 cups of Refined White Sugar (do not substitute)

3 cups of Cake Flour (make sure it's cake flour – not regular or bread)

5 large Eggs

¾ cup of 7-Up

3 tbsp. of imitation vanilla

¼ tbsp. of almond or lemon extract

½ tsp. of lemon zest

Chocolate or vanilla icing

Bundt cake pan

Optional Extras: ½ cup of Raspberry Jam, OR ½ cup melted semi-sweet chocolate, ½ teaspoon orange flavoring, chocolate cooking chips

Method

1. Grease Bundt Cake pan. Sprinkle with Cake Flour and Coat. Set aside in cool place.

2. Preheat oven to 350º.

3. Beat softened butter with sugar until creamy and white.

4. Add flavorings and lemon zest and mix thoroughly.

5. While mixing – slowly add about ¼ cup of Cake Flour.

6. Beat until smooth.

7. While mixing, slowly add 1 egg.

8. Beat until smooth.

9. While mixing – slowly add ¼ cup of cake flour.

10. Beat until smooth. ➪

---

11. While mixing, slowly add about 2 tbsp. of 7up.

12. Beat until smooth.

13. Repeat this pattern – ¼ cup of flour, beat, 1 egg, beat, ¼ cup of flour, beat, a little 7-UP, beat. Do Not Try To Add all ingredients at once, as this will make the mixture gummy and too tough.

14. When all ingredients have been incorporated, pour mixture in Bundt pan. Make sure the batter is spread evenly.

15. If adding extras: orange flavoring – at Step 4 – add the vanilla flavoring, lemon and orange flavoring and orange zest. Do Not Add any almond flavoring if adding orange!

16. If adding extras raspberry jam and or melted semi-sweet chocolate: When all cake ingredients are mixed, pour ½ of cake mixture in Bundt pan. Spoon in the raspberry jam and or melted semi-sweet chocolate. This can be dropped by spoonful and then take a knife and swirl the jam/chocolate in the top part of mixture. Don't do deep mixing- just do as if frosting a cake. Pour rest of cake mixture on top and bake.

17. If adding extra Chocolate Chips – when all ingredients have been incorporated FOLD in about ½ cup of small bittersweet chocolate chips into mixture. Do not BEAT. Mixture will be light and creamy so remember chocolate chips are heavy so do not add a lot.

18. Bake cake in preheated oven for 1 hour 10 minutes.

19. Check for doneness in the center with a toothpick.

20. Let cake cool on cake rack or area where air will get to cake from top and bottom.

21. Turn cake over onto cake pan or display area.

22. Heat prepared icing and drizzle over cake.

23. Cover with glass or plastic covering and set aside for at least 4 hours for cake flavours to settle. Glass or plastic also retains the moisture so that the cake literally melts in your mouth while eating.

24. Serve alone or with fresh fruit in season with milk or hot tea.

Glazed Icing
– Mahasin D. Shamsid-Deen

Ingredients

2 cups confectioners' sugar, sift before measuring

1 ½ tbsp. soft butter

1 tsp. vanilla

½ tsp. salt

3 to 4 tbsp. of milk

Optional

2 tbsp. of Cocoa for chocolate icing

1 tbsp. of softened cream cheese

½ tsp. orange flavoring or 2 tsp. orange juice

Method

1. Combine all icing ingredients in small mixing bowl.
2. Stir until smooth and well blended.
3. Adjust for spreading consistency if necessary, adding more milk or more confectioners' sugar. Heat and Drizzle on cake when done.
4. Add Cocoa for Chocolate glaze.
5. Add cream cheese and orange flavoring for Orange glaze.
6. Orange glaze icing is appropriate for all versions of cake – plain, raspberry or chocolate chip.

Sweet Potato Pie
– Amel S. Abdullah

Ingredients

Crust:

1½ cups white all-purpose flour

½ cup shredded coconut

¼ cup sugar

1 stick butter, softened

Filling

4 cups mashed sweet potatoes

4 eggs

1 ½ cups evaporated milk

1 ½ cups brown sugar

¼ tsp. salt

3 tbsp. flour

½ tsp. vanilla

1 tsp. ground cinnamon

¼ tsp. ground ginger

¼ tsp. ground cloves

Whipped cream (optional)

Method

1. Preheat oven to 350° F.

2. In a 9 x 13 in Pyrex baking-dish, mix together the ingredients for the crust.

3. With your hands, press the mixture into the bottom of the dish, so that it is spread out evenly. Spread some of the mixture up the sides of the dish as well to form a shallow crust.

4. Bake for 10 minutes and remove from oven.

5. While the crust is baking, mix together the ingredients for the filling in a bowl.

6. Pour the mixture into the warm crust once it has been removed from the oven.

7. Bake for 1 hour at 350° F.

8. Allow the pie to cool down to room temperature and then place into the refrigerator until chilled.

9. If desired, serve topped with whipped cream.

Maʼmoul (cookie-pastry)

– Balqees Mohammed

This recipe has three Steps. Step 1 is preparation of the filling mixture, Step 2 is preparation of the pastry dough, and Step 3 is combining the ingredients for baking.

To create this recipe you will need: cookie sheets, a pastry decorative press, an electric mixer, and several sizes of bowls.

Step 1:
Filling Ingredients

½ - 1 lb. pitted dates

1-2 tbsp. cooking oil

3-4 tsp. pre-browned sesame seeds

2 tsp. green fennel seeds

2 tsp. caraway seeds

Topping: (optional)

1-2 cup powdered sugar

Filling Method

1. Place ½ to 1 lb. of pitted dates (the soft dark type) in an open saucepan or fry pan.
2. Add 1-2 tbsp. cooking oil or butter and turn with wooden spoon consistently over heat for 2-3 minutes.
3. Take the pan off the fire, let cool slightly.
4. Optional - add pre-browned sesame seeds, caraway seeds and fennel seeds to the date mixture.
5. Spoon the date mixture (complete with oil and seeds) out onto a plate or bowl, and set aside to cool while you prepare the dough mixture.

Step 2:
Pastry Dough Ingredients

3 eggs

3 sticks of butter (or equivalent to ¾ lbs. preferably butter or margarine, but vegetable shortening will do)

½ cup fine white sugar

3-4 cups flour (all white, or a mixture of brown or cracked wheat and white)

2 tsp. baking powder

1 tsp. vanilla flavoring

½ cup coarsely chopped nuts (peanuts or pistachios) *optional ⇨

Pastry Dough Method

1. Cream together the eggs, butter and sugar with electric mixer for about 2-3 minutes on high speed, or with wooden spoon, until thoroughly mixed into a creamy texture.

2. Add flour, baking powder and vanilla.

3. Mix with mixer for as long as it will work, and then add remaining flour (or additional flour, as needs may indicate) mixing with wooden spoon. The final mixture of the dough should be stiff enough that even the wooden spoon does not work easily, and you need to use your hands for mixing, but soft enough that it is not workable to roll out on a surface. *

4. Place the mixed pastry dough in a bowl.

*Note 1 - About Pastry Dough Consistency - For those familiar with drop cookies (such as chocolate chip, etc.), the final dough should be similar in consistency, yet slightly stiffer. Once mixed, you can test the dough by washing and drying your hands thoroughly, and test it with one finger. If it comes out with dough sticking to it, the dough needs more flour. If it comes out clean, then it is most likely all right for making the pastries.

**Note 2 - You can try this method, of powdering the pastry press with flour, or moistening it with oil. Whichever method works best, then use that for your own process. Just remember that if you opt to use flour in the press, use it sparingly, for you don't want too much dry flour on the surface of the pastry as you go for baking. And if you use oil, the same warning applies, for too much oil on the surface of the pastry may cause cracking during baking. You need just enough (of either flour or oil) on the inner surface of the press to help ease the removal of the pastry once it is pressed.

Step 3:

Making and Baking Pastries Method

1. Be sure your hands are thoroughly washed and dried before beginning the next step.

2. Organize pastry dough, filling, pastry press and cooking sheets:

   • Partially fill one small bowl with cooking oil. It will be used for moistening your hands as you work with the dough.

   • Partially fill one small bowl with flour. It will be used for preparing the bowl in which you will place the prepared pastry, in order to allow for easy and quick removal from the bowl.

- The bowl of mixed pastry dough
- The bowl of cooled date mixture
- Cookie sheets, lightly greased
- The pastry decorative press
- Pre-heat oven to 350° F.

3. To begin with, moisten your hands (inner palms sides) with some oil or flour, and then pinch off a small ball of the dough. (Approximately 1-inch diameter)
4. Squeeze it and roll it between your palms until it is a tight ball.
5. Using both palms of your hands, flatten the ball into the palm of one hand.
6. With the empty hand, pinch off a small amount of the date filling mixture (about half as much of the dough), and place it in the center of the flattened out dough.
7. Pinch the edges of the dough to close the filling in the center.
8. Place the ball into your pastry decorative press and press it down hard to ensure the decorative design embeds itself on the one side, while flattening out the other side.
9. When the design is pressed into the dough sufficiently, remove it from the press, and place the pastry flat side down onto your cookie sheet or baking pan. Continue doing this until all the pastry dough and date filling have been combined and are on the cookie sheets.
10. Bake in a pre-heated oven for approximately 10-12 minutes, or until the outer edges (around the bottom side) start turning golden brown. *

**Note* -- You can do a test cookie, if preferred. If, during the baking process, you notice the dough flattening out a bit or the decorative press on the top flattening out, that means that your dough is too soft and needs some more flour. If, during the baking process, the pastry cracks excessively, that means that the dough is too stiff, and you should have taken more precaution in the mixing stage, adding the flour smaller bits at a time. Some cracking is normal and acceptable, but excessive cracking is a sign that your dough is too stiff.

Options

1. Incorporate chopped nuts into the pastry by pressing the filled ball into finely chopped nuts before you press it into the decorative press.
2. Before serving, and once fully cooled, you can dip the finished cookies into some powdered sugar. ⇨

Note – Do not try to eat or serve this cookie/pastry while hot because the date filling becomes very hot while baking, and may burn your tongue or lips if eaten while fresh out of the oven. These cookies will keep well for several weeks, if kept in firmly tight plastic containers.

The Holy Qur'an 6:141 It is He Who produceth gardens, with trellises and without, and dates, and tilth with produce of all kinds, and olives and pomegranates, similar (in kind) and different (in variety): eat of their fruit in their season.

Zucchini Bread

– Maryam O. Funmilayo

Ingredients

3 cups of flour

3 eggs

1 cup of honey

¾ cup vegetable oil

1 tsp. non-alcoholic pure vanilla extract

2 cups of grated zucchini

1 cup of nuts or raisins

1 tsp. cinnamon

1 tsp. salt

1 tsp. baking soda

1 tsp. baking powder

½ cup sour cream

Method

1. Mix everything together in a bowl except the nuts or raisins.

2. Add the nuts or raisins at the very end.

3. Bake in 2 separate bread pans at 350 degrees for 1 hour.

Serves 6 to 8 people

A toothsome slice of zucchini bread is enough to make you feel satiated!

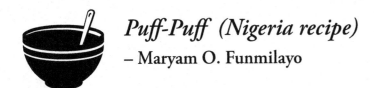

Puff-Puff *(Nigeria recipe)*
– Maryam O. Funmilayo

Ingredients

2 cups of whole-wheat flour

2 cups of water

½ cup of pure cane raw sugar

2 tsp. of yeast

Vegetable oil for deep-frying

Method

1. Mix the whole-wheat flour, raw sugar, water, and yeast together in a medium-sized bowl until the batter is smooth.

2. Cover with a moist cloth or aluminum foil for 2 hours so that the dough can rise.

3. Once the dough has risen, put some vegetable oil into a deep fryer or pot until it is 3 inches high (too little oil will result in flatter balls instead of bouncing, round balls). Place the deep fryer or pot on low heat for few minutes.

4. Test to make sure the oil is hot enough by putting a tiny drop of batter into the oil. If it is not hot enough, the batter will stay at the bottom of the pot rather than rising to the top.

5. When the oil is hot enough, use a spatula to dish up the batter. Use another spatula to drop it in the oil. Make sure the batter is dropped in the hot oil in the shape of a ball.

6. Fry for a few minutes until the bottom side is golden brown.

7. Turn the ball over and fry for a few more minutes until the other side is golden brown.

8. Use a perforated spatula to take the puff-puff out of the oil one by one.

9. Place them directly on a napkin and a plate so that the napkin can soak up some of the excess oil.

If you wish, you can sprinkle some cinnamon powder on the puff-puff to add another kind of different, sweet flavor.

Frying time: 30 minutes
Makes: 40-60 balls
Simply palatable!

Mixed Berry Parfait
– Sabah Negash

Ingredients

Low fat yogurt

½ cup fresh chopped strawberries

½ cup fresh blueberries

Low fat granola

Whipped Topping

Maraschino Cherries

Method

1. Mix chopped strawberries and blueberries together with a small amount of sugar.
2. Take a parfait glass or other tall glass. Spoon two tablespoons of yogurt into the cup.
3. Layer two spoonfuls of mixed berries.
4. Sprinkle granola on top.
5. Continue the process of layering the yogurt, berries and granola.
6. Finish your dessert with whipped topping and a Maraschino cherry.

Makes four servings.

Comments: I have never been one to like fresh fruits in my dessert. But I was blown away by this simple yet yummy fresh treat I had at a friend's some time ago. I have tried it with a variety of flavored yogurts but I really like it with vanilla yogurt because it does not overpower or take away from the taste of the fresh berries.

Saqudanah

This dessert is made with saqudanah, which is similar to tapioca and is actually palletized sago. Saqudanah is sold in supermarkets or spice stores.

Ingredients

½ cup saqudanah

6 cups milk

¾ cup sugar

½ tsp. rose water

¼ cup raisins

3 tbsp. shredded almonds

Method

1. Wash the saqudanah in a colander.

2. In a pot, pour milk, add saqudanah and raisins and bring to a boil.

3. Simmer for 30 minutes, stirring constantly.

4. Add sugar and cook for 10 minutes.

5. Remove from heat, cool and pour into a bowl.

6. Add almonds and rose water.

7. Refrigerate and serve cool.

The consistency should be similar to that of soup, not too thick. Milk can be added according to individual taste.

Strawberry Nut Bread

Ingredients

3 cups flour

1 tsp. salt

1 tbsp. cinnamon

1 tsp. baking soda

2 cups sugar

3 eggs, slightly beaten

1 ¼ cup vegetable oil

3 cups fresh strawberries, mashed

1 cup chopped nuts

Method

1. Preheat oven to 350 degrees F.
2. Grease 2 loaf pans.
3. Combine all dry ingredients in a large bowl and mix well, make a well and add rest of ingredients just until moistened.
4. Pour into loaf pans, sprinkle tops with cinnamon-sugar.
5. Bake one hour until done.

Bread Crumbs Pudding/Payasum

Ingredients

2 cups bread crumbs

1 cup milk

1 ½ cups cashew nuts & raisins

¾ cup sugar

5 tsp. Ghee

Food color and rose water (optional)

Method

1. In a pan take 2 spoons of ghee and fry the cashews and raisins.
2. When done add the unsalted breadcrumbs and fry for few minutes.
3. Add milk and cook for 10 minutes on a low flame.
4. When ½ cooked, add the sugar, food color and the remaining ghee.
5. When cooled add little rose water and serve chilled.
6. Garnish with saffron Tortilla Wafers

Grandma's Sugar Cookies
– Linda D. Delgado

Ingredients

2 cups white flour

1 tsp. baking powder

¾ tsp. salt

½ cup soft butter or margarine

1 cup of sugar

2 eggs

1 tsp. almond flavoring

1½ cups chopped walnuts or pecans

Method

1. Combine flour, salt and baking powder.
2. With an electric mixer at medium-low speed, beat the butter and sugar until light and fluffy.
3. Beat in egg and almond flavoring.
4. Slowly stir in flour and chopped nuts until well mixed (dough may be slightly sticky).
5. Place the mixture on plastic or foil paper, wrap tightly and refrigerate for an hour or two or even overnight. (Cookie dough will keep in the refrigerator for up to one week.)
6. Remove the dough from foil. Squeeze off ⅓ of the dough.
7. Smooth into a ball and place on a flat surface covered in flour.
8. With a rolling pin, roll the dough to one-inch thickness. The dough should be in the shape of a flat circle.
9. With cookie cutters of your choice, cut the dough and then place the cutout cookies on an ungreased cookie sheet.
10. Bake in a preheated oven of 350°F for 8 to 10 minutes, or until the bottom of the cookies are golden brown.
11. Cool for 30 minutes - then frost each Cookie Q with butter crème frosting.
12. Add coconut, colored sprinkles, or colored sugar for decorations.

Maple Pumpkin Pie

Ingredients

1 ¼ cups maple syrup

1 tsp. salt

4 large eggs

1 29 oz. can of unseasoned pumpkin

2½ cups evaporated milk (1) 12 oz. can and (1) 8 oz. can.

2 - 9 inch deep dish unbaked pie shells (4 c. volume) or

4 - 9 inch shallow unbaked pie shells (2 cup volume)

*You can use a graham cracker crust.

Spice Mix

Option A

1 tbsp. to 2 tbsp. store bought pumpkin pie spice

Option B

2 tsp. to 1 tsp. ground cinnamon

1 tsp. to 1 ½ tsp. ground ginger

½ tsp. to ¾ tsp. ground cloves

1/8 to ¼ tsp. Allspice

Method

1. Mix: maple syrup, salt, spice mix, in small bowl. Set aside.
2. Beat: 4 eggs in large bowl.
3. Stir In: syrup and spice mix into eggs.
4. Stir In: pumpkin into egg mix.
5. Gradually Stir In: evaporated milk.
6. Pour: into pie shells.
7. Bake: 425 degrees Fahrenheit for 15 minutes.
8. Reduce Temperature: to 350 degrees Fahrenheit.
9. Continue Baking: 4-cup volume pie shells for 40-50 minutes, until knife inserted near center comes out clean.
10. 2-cup volume pie shells for 20-30 minutes, until knife inserted near center comes out clean.
11. Cool: on wire rack, 90 minutes to 2 hours.

Serve immediately after cooling -or- refrigerate.

The Holy Qur'an: 2:61 And remember ye said: "O Moses! we cannot endure one kind of food (always); so beseech thy Lord for us to produce for us of what the earth growth, -its pot-herbs, and cucumbers, Its garlic, lentils, and onions."

Chocolate Filled Thumbprint Cookies

Ingredients

1 cup butter

1 cup brown sugar

2 tsp. vanilla

3 cups flour

½ cup chocolate chips (Mini chips are best)

2 tbsp. milk

½ tsp. salt

½ cup powdered sugar

Method

1. Cream together the butter and brown sugar. Stir in the milk and vanilla.

2. Add the flour and salt, then the chocolate chips. It will be very stiff dough.

3. Form into balls that are about the size of walnuts. Place on an ungreased cookie sheet about 2" apart.

4. Press your thumb into each ball of dough. This will make the depression that will hold the filling.

5. Bake at 350 degrees for 15 minutes, or until light golden brown. Remove from baking sheet, cool slightly and roll in powdered sugar, OR use a sieve and dust the cookies with powdered sugar--less messy!

6. When cool, put a generous ½ tsp. of chocolate filling (below) in each cookie.

Chocolate Filling Ingredients

1 ¾ cups chocolate chips

2 tbsp. shortening (Crisco)

¼ cup corn syrup

2 tbsp. water

1 tsp. vanilla

Method

1. In the microwave in a glass microwave safe 4 cup measure or bowl, melt together the chocolate chips, shortening, and corn syrup. Heat for 1 minute at a time, and stir occasionally, watching carefully that it does not boil over.

2. Stir in the water and vanilla so that all is well combined.

3. Cool for 5 minutes, and then fill each cookie.

It helps to chill the cookies in the fridge to set the filling, before you put them away. Once the filling has chilled and set, it will not melt at room temperature. Makes about 3 dozen cookies. It is not a typo: this cookie contains no baking powder or soda, and no eggs.

The Holy Qur'an 2:172 O ye who believe! Eat of the good things that We have provided for you, and be grateful to Allah, if it is Him ye worship.

Brownies to Die For

Ingredients

1 cup flour

¼ tsp. baking soda

¼ tsp. salt

5 tbsp. butter

¾ cup sugar

2 tbsp. of water or cold coffee

1-6 or 8 oz. package chocolate chips.
(Use real chocolate chips--not the imitation flavored)

1 tsp. vanilla

2 eggs

½ cup chopped walnuts (optional)

Method

1. Preheat oven to 325 degrees F.

2. Grease an 8" or 9" square pan.

3. In a medium saucepan, combine the butter, sugar, and liquid. Bring just to a boil. Remove pan from heat.

4. Add the bag of chocolate chips to the butter/sugar mixture and stir until the chips melt.

5. Add the eggs, one at a time and beat after each addition.

6. Gradually blend in the flour, soda and salt. Add the nuts if you're using them. Spread the mixture in the prepared pan.

7. Bake 30-35 minutes--do not over-bake.

Cool completely before cutting. Makes a 9"x9" pan.

Chocolate & Honey Flapjacks
– Amina Malik

Ingredients

  1½ cups rolled porridge oats

  ¼ cup butter

  ¼ cup brown sugar

  3 tbsp. honey

  1 tbsp. sunflower oil

  ¾ cup plain chocolate

Method

1. Preheat the oven to 300°F.

2. In a pan on the stove add the butter, sugar and honey and heat through gently. Continue until the butter has melted and the sugar is no longer visible.

3. Remove from the heat and stir in the oats.

4. Grease a 12" x 8" x 1½" rectangular tin.

5. Fill the tin with the mixture. Press the mixture down using a spatula until evenly spread.

6. Bake on the middle shelf of an oven for 40-45 minutes or until golden brown. Leave to rest in the tin until completely cool.

7. Meanwhile, melt the chocolate in a heatproof bowl over a pan of hot water. Add the oil, mixing this in well.

8. Pour the chocolate over the chilled flapjack base.

9. Leave to cool in the refrigerator. Once the chocolate has set, score a grid across the tin lightly with a knife and then cut into squares.

Makes 12 squares.

Halal Choc-Marshmallow Cupcakes
– Amina Malik

Growing up in a town with few Muslims meant poor access to halal products. Marshmallows were one of a few things I could not eat as they are made using non-halal animal by-product. Now, however, halal marshmallows are available all across the UK. Here's a delicious recipe I love to make as a special treat for all the children in the family – using the coveted marshmallows I could not have as a kid myself!

Ingredients for Cupcakes

1-1¼ cups plain flour

1 tsp. baking powder

½ tsp. baking soda

1 cup unsalted butter, cubed

⅞ cup white granulated sugar

2 large eggs

4½ tsp. plain cocoa powder

½ cup boiling water

¼ tsp. salt

1 tsp. pure vanilla extract

½ cup of milk

Ingredients for Marshmallow Frosting

1¼ cups unsalted butter, cubed

5 cups confectioners' sugar

1 tbsp. vanilla extract

1 tbsp. milk

Halal mini marshmallows

Any plain chocolate, grated for decoration (optional)

Method for cupcakes

Preheat the oven to 350°F

1. Mix the flour, baking powder, baking soda, cocoa powder and salt.

2. In a separate bowl beat the butter until smooth using a hand mixer.

3. Add the sugar and beat again until the sugar and butter are fully combined and the mixture is creamy.

4. Add one egg at a time and beat the mixture again after each one.

5. Add the vanilla extract.

6. Add the flour mixture to this bowl and combine thoroughly so that the entire mixture is brown. Any uncombined parts now will be visible in your cupcakes later.

7. Spoon the mixture into the paper cases until two-thirds full.

8. Place rack in centre of oven.

9. Bake in the preheated oven for 20–25 minutes. The cupcakes should be golden brown. Leave the cupcakes to cool on a wire rack.

Method for Marshmallow Frosting

1. In a large bowl and using a mixer, beat the butter until smooth.

2. Add the confectioners' sugar, 1 cup at a time beating until smooth.

3. Add the vanilla and 1 tbsp. milk. Beat until fluffy. If the mixture looks dry add a second tbsp. of milk.

4. Add halal mini marshmallows and fold into mixture.

5. One the cupcakes are cool, use a tablespoon to smooth the frosting on top.

6. Sprinkle grated chocolate over the frosting to decorate and serve.

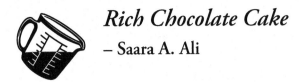

Rich Chocolate Cake
– Saara A. Ali

Ingredients

1½ cups flour

⅓ cup cocoa powder

1 tsp. baking soda

¼ tsp. salt

1 cup sugar

½ cup olive oil

1 cup cold water

2 tsp. vanilla essence

2 tsp. vinegar

Method

1. Preheat oven to 350ºF (180ºC). Grease and line an 8 in. pan.
2. Combine flour, cocoa powder, baking soda, salt and sugar in a bowl.
3. Whisk together olive oil, cold water, vanilla essence and vinegar in another bowl.
4. Stir wet ingredients into dry ingredients. Mix until well combined. Beat mixture with spoon for about 1 minute.
5. Pour into a pan and bake for 25 minutes or until done.
6. Cool and top with frosting of your choice.

Makes one 8-inch cake.

Note – This recipe does not contain eggs. You may substitute olive oil for vegetable oil. To give a richer flavor use brewed coffee in place of water.

Bean Pie

– Umm Juwayrriyah

This is a favorite dessert among Urban African-Americans. You can use white canned navy beans. Traditionally dried beans were used. People would boil them for hours, but I haven't tasted a difference with the canned beans.

Ingredients

2 cups of cooked navy white beans or 1 can of navy white beans

1 stick butter

2 tbsp. flour

4 eggs

1 tsp. nutmeg

2 cups sugar

1 14oz. can evaporated milk

1 tsp. cinnamon

2 tbsp. vanilla

2 or 3 ready-made pie shells

Method

1. Cook beans until soft. Preheat oven to 350 degrees.
2. In electric blender blend beans, butter, milk, eggs, nutmeg and flour about 2 minutes on medium speed.
3. Pour mixture into a large mixing bowl.
4. Add sugar and vanilla. Mix well.
5. Pour into pie shells.
6. Bake about one hour until golden brown.

Makes 2 or 3 Bean Pies.

Specialties

Egyptian Eggplant Pickles
– Judith Nelson Eldawy

Ingredients

2 lbs. of small white eggplants

20 -25 big cloves of garlic

1 or 2 green peppers, diced-depending on size

¼ cup salt

1 tbsp. Cumin

Olive Oil

Vinegar

3-4 Fresh lemons or limes

½ tbsp. hot red pepper, powdered or crushed

Method

1. These are very easy to make. Wash eggplants well and cut the tops with stems off.

2. Make an incision from top of the eggplant to ⅔ of the way down.

3. Boil in salted water until they have changed color to grey, about 10 minutes.

4. Drain eggplants and let them cool.

5. With a mortar and pestle, crush garlic cloves and green pepper.

6. When these are coarsely crushed, add about a ¼-cup or a bit more of salt to mortar along with a tablespoon of cumin and a couple pinches of red hot pepper.

7. Mix well with pestle until you have a paste.

8. In a large dish that has a tight fitting cover, drizzle olive oil in the bottom.

9. Take one eggplant and squeeze lemon/lime juice along the inside as well as outside of it.

10. Scoop up a small amount of garlic paste on the tip of your finger and spread this along both sides of the inside of the eggplant.

11. Press sides together. If the eggplant has separated in 2 pieces, spread the paste on the inside and roll it up.

12. Place eggplant in dish and repeat above steps until all the eggplant is gone.

13. Over every layer, drizzle a little olive oil and vinegar over the eggplant in the dish.

This can be eaten immediately and should keep for about a month.
Makes about 24 servings. ⇨

Note – Pickles, called turshi in Arabic, are compliments to every meal, including breakfast. They can be made from practically any vegetable, in addition to lemons.

The Holy Qur'an, 107:1-3 "Have you ever considered (the kind of person) who denies the Judgment (to come)? Behold, it is (the one) who repulses the orphan (with harshness) and feels no urge to feed the needy."

Fish Fritters (or Accra from Trinidad & Tobago)
– Saara A. Ali

Add a salad to go along with your *Accra* for a light lunch.

Ingredients

½ lb. salted fish

1 tsp. lemon juice

1 cup finely chopped green onions

1 tsp. finely chopped garlic

½ tsp. hot pepper sauce (optional)

2 cups flour

2 tsp. baking powder

½ cup water

1½ cups oil (for frying)

Method

1. Place salted fish in cool water and slowly bring to a gentle boil. Turn off heat and let fish soak in water until cool.

2. Remove fish from pot, rinse in several changes of cool water. Drain and pat dry. Flake the fish into small pieces.

3. In a bowl, combine fish, lemon juice, finely chopped green onions, finely chopped garlic and if using, hot pepper sauce. Stir well.

4. Add flour, baking powder and enough water to make a soft and somewhat sticky batter. (Note this mixture is never dry and smooth like bread dough).

5. Heat oil in a frying pan until medium-high temperature.

6. Drop batter by the teaspoonful into the hot oil and fry. Keep turning the accras and fry until golden brown (about 2-3 minutes).

7. Drain on paper towels and serve warm as is or with a dip.

Definitions – *Salted Fish* is cod or haddock that has been dried and salted. It does not require refrigeration, though if you are storing it for lengthy periods (it can last for several months) it is advisable to refrigerate it. Salted Fish produces a pungent scent when being boiled but boiling removes the excessive salt used to cure the fish. You can find it in most large supermarkets or in specialty Caribbean or Asian food stores.

Note – No need to add salt to this recipe as the fish imparts its saltiness to the dish. A great dip to make to go with this dish is a tamarind dip. Combine in a blender or food processor: 1 tsp. tamarind pulp, 3 tsp. sugar, ½ tsp. salt, ½ tsp. chopped garlic, ¼ cup water and hot pepper sauce to taste. Makes approximately 15.

Hummus
– Maryam Dana

Ingredients

4 tbsp. tahini

1 lemon squeezed

1½ tsp. salt (or to taste)

1½ tsp. Cumin

2 tins chickpeas (leave some chickpeas for topping)

Olive oil

Chopped long red pepper or sun dried tomatoes (optional)

Method

Blend all ingredients (excluding the red pepper and tomato) together until fine.

Topping Ingredients:

1 Cubed Red Pepper

Sun dried tomato (optional)

Olive oil

Mustard Seeds

Dash of Aroma Chilli or to taste

Dash of Liquid Seasoning or to taste

Dash of Lemon Pepper or to taste

The extra chickpeas from above

Method

1. Heat the olive oil in a pan.
2. Fry the mustard seeds until they start popping.
3. Add the peppers (sun dried tomatoes), chickpeas and spices.
4. Cover and cook on a low heat for a few minutes.
5. Pour over hummus.
6. Add more olive oil if required.

Podina Chutney - (dip)

Ingredients

1 bunch Mint

2 tbsp. Green Chili

1 tsp. Salt

2 tbsp. Pomegranate Seed - dried

3 cups Yogurt

4 tbsp. Water

Method

1. Remove stems from green chilies.

2. Blend together mint, green chilies, and salt and pomegranate seeds in an electric blender to make a paste.

3. Add water to make mixture smooth.

4. Remove from blender and mix in yogurt.

Makes 36 ¼-cup servings

Chicken Stock, Egyptian Style
– Judith Nelson Eldawy

Ingredients

1 whole, well washed large chicken, trimmed of excess skin and fat

1 small ripe tomato

1 medium onion

4-5 large peeled cloves of garlic

Salt

Black pepper

Cumin

3-4 pods of cardamom

Method

1. Add chicken to large pot of water with the tomato and onion.

2. Add a couple tablespoons of salt.

3. After boiling for 10 minutes, skim any fat that is floating on top of boiling stock and throw away.

4. Crush garlic cloves with the flat of a knife and add to the pot along with cardamom pods and about a heaping tablespoon of pepper and cumin and boil for an hour or so, stirring intermittently.

5. Add more water as needed during cooking and adjust seasonings to individual taste.

6. I sometimes add granulated garlic to the broth as well and a handful of fresh, washed coriander leaves, finely chopped, if I am making a vegetable soup instead of the lissan asfour soup.

7. Remove chicken once it is cooked through and fish out cardamom pods and throw them away. What is left is your basic stock.

8. Chicken is divided into pieces, browned in butter or oil and sprinkled with salt, pepper and cumin.

9. One may substitute meat chunks for the chicken if a meat stock is desired-just omit cardamom pods from the recipe.

Note – There is an Egyptian saying, "If the soup is good, the whole dinner will be good." There is a lot of truth to this as the stock is the basis of most Egyptian cooking and is used to flavor tomato sauces and to make vegetable or pasta based soups.

Basic Tomato Sauce, Egyptian Style
– Judith Nelson Eldawy

Ingredients

8-10 ripe, well washed tomatoes

3-4 garlic cloves

1 medium diced onion

Olive oil

Salt

Sugar-couple pinches or cinnamon

Black pepper

Cumin

Granulated garlic

Method

1. Fill a blender with diced tomatoes, garlic cloves and add about ¼ cup of water. Blend well.

2. Sauté onion in a couple tablespoons of olive oil.

3. Once browned, add tomato puree, either strained or not according to preference. I usually don't bother unless a picky in law is watching.

4. Depending on what I am cooking, I add either sugar or cinnamon to cut the acidity of the tomato sauce.

5. Add several ladlefuls of stock and seasonings to taste and simmer for ½ hour or until sauce takes on a deeper color and reduces to desired thickness.

Note – To this sauce, one may add any vegetable or legumes. Peas and carrots, white beans (after soaking overnight), black eyed peas (after soaking a couple hours. You can also boil beans to cook faster, if preferred.), okra and green beans are most common. For zucchini, I would add about a half-cup of washed and dried split chickpea (called hummus) to the sauce and simmer it for the ½-hour sauce is cooking before adding zucchini.

Piaz Pakoras (Onion Fritters)
– Nazli Currin

Ingredients

1 cup Gram flour (besan)

½ tsp. chile powder

½ tsp. cumin seeds

½ tsp. salt

1 tsp. baking powder

1 green chile thinly sliced

1 cup finely chopped cilantro

1 large or 2 medium onions

Enough water to make a thick batter.

Enough oil for deep-frying

Method

1. Peel the onions, cut thick rings and keep aside.

2. In a bowl, mix all the dry ingredients and the chopped green chilies and cilantro.

3. Pour water to make a thick batter (pancake consistency).

4. Heat oil and dip onion rings to coat well & deep fry on medium heat to a golden brown color.

5. Serve with mint and cilantro chutney (see next page).

Note – Any other vegetables can be used instead of onions: Potato, zucchini, eggplant, cauliflower, broccoli, etc.

Mint and Cilantro Chutney
– Nazli Currin

Ingredients

20 leaves of fresh mint

1 cup fresh cilantro

2 green Jalapeno chills

1 ½ tbsp. lemon juice

Salt to taste

(Optional) 1 tbsp. roasted sesame seeds

Water

Method

Blend altogether with enough water to make chutney with the consistency of ketchup or a little less thick.

Drinks

Simple Cardamom Tea
– Sabah Negash

I first learned to use cardamom in foods and drinks when my sisters and I studied Arabic in Sudan. My mother loved Sudanese tea and she got the ingredients from a good friend to make it, cardamom being one of them.

Barely new to city of Khartoum, with very little knowledge of the language, we decided to take our first solo trip to the souk. So, off to the local farmers market we went in search of cardamom, sugar and tea and other items on our grocery list. As our bags filled with items, it came time to purchase the spices we needed. My sisters did not know the Arabic word for cardamom at the time and I vaguely remembered it from my mom's friend. After a few minutes of discussion between each other, we asked the seller for, "hamamaan." His initial expression was priceless. It was a mix of disbelief, shock, and utter confusion. He asked us for clarification and we said, "Hamamaan? Shai?" The guy burst into laughter once he realized what we were asking for. He picked up a small sack of cardamom pods and said, "Habbahaan." Apparently, "hamamaan" meant "two bathrooms."

In Sudan, tea drinking is a very important part of their lives, socially and culturally. When you visit someone, you are usually offered tea. Red tea is often offered around lunch and dinnertime. But if you happen to visit during the mid-morning hours, you are bound to get milk tea.

Ingredients

7 cups of water

5 cardamom pods

2 teabags

Sugar to taste

Milk optional

Method

1. Put the water and cardamom pods in a saucepan and bring to a boil.

2. Turn off the heat.

3. Add teabags to the boiled water and cardamom.

4. Let stand for few minutes until tea turns red.

5. Remove teabags before the tea becomes bitter.

6. Strain tea and add sugar to taste.

Spicy Orange Cider
– Sabah Negash

Here is a tasty drink sure to keep you warm through the winter and loaded with essential vitamins to keep you healthy.

Ingredients

⅛ tsp. powdered nutmeg

½ cinnamon stick

2 tbsp. chopped/minced ginger

2 cups water

2 cups orange juice

Method

1. Combine the garlic, nutmeg, cinnamon stick and ginger in a pot. Add two cups of water and bring to a boil.

2. Let the water boil till only ½ cup of liquid is left in the pot.

3. Add the orange juice to the pot and heat for two minutes.

4. Turn off the heat and cover the pot for four minutes.

5. Strain the spicy orange cider into a mug and enjoy!

Cherry Limeade

Ingredients

1 cup Sprite

¼ cup cherry juice (Libby brand is good)

2-3 lime wedges (each ⅛ lime)

Method

Pour Sprite into a glass over ice.

Add cherry juice.

Add 2-3 lime wedges, squeezing slightly before dropping each one in

Serves 1

The Holy Qur'an 14:38 "Our Lord! You truly know all that we may hide [in our hearts] as well as all that we bring into the open, for nothing whatever, be it on earth or in heaven, remains hidden from Allah."

Saudi Champaigne
– Balqees Mohammed

Although the name of this drink has the word 'champaigne' in it, it is not a form of liquor. Having begun it's fame in only the most elegant of restaurants around the Kingdom of Saudi Arabia, it has become so popular that it is regularly found on the menus of more than only the restaurants of the five star hotels. It is very easy to make, and adopts itself to readily available substitutes for the ingredients, and is quite refreshing with any meal, or on its own.

Ingredients

- 1 quart Grape Juice (the red juice is best)
- 1 quart Apple Cider
- 1 pint Perrier (or any other similar carbonated water)
- 1 pint (or 1 small bottle/can) non-alcoholic beer
- 1 apple (cleaned but not skinned, sliced horizontally)
- 1 lemon (same preparation method as for the apple)
- 2-3 sprigs fresh mint (leaves remain on stem)

Method

1. In large mixing bowl or large pitcher, pour equal amounts of the grape juice and apple cider (begin with only a half of each of the juices), add the Perrier (or carbonated water) and the non-alcoholic beer. If there is still enough room left in the pitcher, add more of the juices, equal amounts of each, until the pitcher is nearly full.

2. Drop the fruit slices into the juice mixture, saving two or three of the lemon slices for garnish around the top of the pitcher (cut halfway into the slice and place on the edge of the pitcher). Clean the mint sprigs (leave leaves attached to the stems) and add these to the mixture. Keep chilled until serving, and stir only slightly.

Do not mix too far ahead of time for serving, or the sparkly texture of the carbonated ingredients will fade.

Take care when pouring into separate glasses that only the liquid pours out, keeping the fruit and mint in the pitcher.

This mixture should serve at least four people, with enough left for refills.

Mint Tea

– Balqees Mohammed

Although this beverage is called "mint tea", there is no tea actually in the ingredients. It is a tea of only mint, and therefore the resulting name being "mint tea" rather than "tea with mint". An excellent remedy for tummy aches and flatulence (bloating).

Ingredients

10-15 sprigs of fresh mint, leaves attached to the stems

2 quarts water

Sugar (optional)

Saffron (optional)

Method

1. Prepare the fresh mint by washing the sprigs, leaving the leaves attached to the stems. Cut off any obviously damaged area of both the leaves and the stems, but no need to cut the leaves off, or to chop.

2. Place the sprigs of mint into a teapot, pour on top of it boiling hot water, leaving enough room for the liquid to boil freely without spilling over. Bring to a boil, then turn the heat down and let simmer on light boil for about ten minutes, or until the liquid becomes a light yellow-green color. If a lot of liquid has evaporated, or you simply want a full pot for serving, add more boiling hot water to the pot.

If you desire a sweet beverage, then add the sugar (to taste –approximately ¼ cup for a 2-quart pot) at the boiling stage for thorough infusion. If not, then simply serve with sugar bowl on the side.

You can add a few threads of saffron at the boiling stage if desired. This will ensure a deeper yellow tint and added flavor to the beverage.

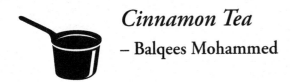

Cinnamon Tea
– Balqees Mohammed

As with the "mint tea", this is a beverage not actually containing any tea in it at all. It is a beverage made of cinnamon alone, hence the name "cinnamon tea", rather than "tea with cinnamon". This is a good remedy to help with lower abdominal cramps, in particular that afflicting women at times of PMS or during menstruation, or after childbirth. It is also an excellent warmer-upper in cold weather.

Ingredients

Cinnamon: 5-6 large sticks or 3 tbsp. of ground cinnamon

2 quarts water

Sugar (optional)

Method

1. Place cinnamon and 1 quart of boiling hot water into teapot, and bring to a boil.
2. Turn the heat down and let simmer on a slow boil for about 10 minutes.
3. Remove from heat, add remaining water, or as much as the pot will hold.
4. If you desire a sweet beverage, then add the sugar at the first boiling stage (about ¼ cup should suffice for a 2 quart pot). If not, then serve sugar bowl on the side.

Note: If using ground cinnamon, the resulting beverage will have a cloudy appearance and perhaps darker than that which is prepared using only bark. If you use the bark, then the resulting beverage will be more clear, similar to any tea. You can use a mixture of both bark and ground, but not necessary to use as much of the ground in this case.

Measurement Conversions

How to Convert Temperature Measurements

Several different temperature scales exist - the Celsius scale sets freezing and boiling points of water at 0 and 100, respectively, while the Fahrenheit scale sets them at 32 and 212. Here's how to convert between the two types.

Multiply the Celsius temperature reading by 9/5, and then add 32 to get the temperature in Fahrenheit: (9/5 * C) + 32 = F

Subtract 32 from the Fahrenheit temperature, and then multiply this quantity by 5/9 to get the temperature in Celsius: (F ' 32) * 5/9 = C.

An easier way to remember temperature conversions is to use estimates, such as 2 for 9/5. For example, multiply temperature in Celsius by 2, and then add 32 to get the approximate temperature in Fahrenheit.

Convert Measurements Between U.S. and Metric Systems

One ounce equals about 28 grams (28.350 g).

1 gram equals 0.035 ounce

Sixteen ounces equal 1 pound.

One pound equals 0.45 kilograms.

1 kilogram equals 2.2 pounds

Liquid Measurements

Three tsps. equal 1 tbsp.

Sixteen tbsp. equal 1 cup

Eight fluid ounces equal 1 cup

Two cups equal 1 pint

Two pints equal 1 quart.

Four quarts equal 1 gallon

⇨

Convert Between U.S. and Metric Systems

One tsp. equals about 5 milliliters

One tbsp. equals about 15 milliliters

One fluid ounce equals about 30 milliliters (29.573 ml)

One cup equals about 240 milliliters (236.584 ml)

One quart equals about 1 liter (0.94635 L)

One gallon equals about 4 liters (3.7854 L)

Section II – Herbs, Cooking Tips, and Healthy Eating Articles

Disclaimers:

Articles and external links published in this book do not necessarily represent the views of Muslim Writers Publishing or the Islamic Writers Alliance, Inc. None of the content of this book is intended to be taken as medical or nutritional advice. Muslim Writers Publishing and the Islamic Writers Alliance, Inc. are not responsible for any health issues which may arise from the usage of any ingredients written about in this book. Medical professionals should be consulted for any serious illness.

Herbs

Cayenne
– Judith Nelson Eldawy

A person who loves spicy foods is familiar with the kick cayenne gives any dish. This member of the pepper family has been heating up global cuisine for centuries. As an herbal remedy, it has a reputation for fighting the congestion of colds, aiding digestion, stimulating circulation and being a painkiller.

The active component in cayenne is capsacin, which is in the oil of the pepper. It can cause a burning sensation and skin irritation, so it is not surprising the self-defense people adopted its use in commercial pepper sprays. Scientists found that capsacin has the ability to interfere with Substance P, which is how the body sends pain signals to the brain.

Taken internally as a tea or in standardized pill form, cayenne helps increase blood circulation, decrease congestion, stimulate digestive juices and speed the healing of ulcers. Used as a diluted nasal wash or a gargle, it relieves sore throats and unblocks sinuses.

However, its best-known use is as a creme. There are many commercial preparations of capsacin cremes and they are used to relieve pain of arthritis, diabetic neuropathy, shingles, pain from amputations, fibromyalgia and headaches. It is also useful for relieving symptoms of Raynauds Disease and in decreasing itching of psoriasis. The last use is possible because the itching sensation and pain sensation follow the same nerve pathways.

Cayenne is safe to use with many ailments but always check with your physician before using it or any herbal supplements. It is important to note that capsacin will severely irritate eyes and other mucous membrane areas. It should not be used in these areas or on open wounds. Wash hands thoroughly with soap and water to remove residue after applying creme or working with the fresh pepper.

Ginger
– Judith Nelson Eldawy

Ginger (Zingiber Officinale) has been used as a culinary flavoring and herbal remedy since ancient times. The Greeks and the Chinese were well aware of its benefits for halting nausea and reducing inflammation.

Numerous modern day scientific trials have confirmed the efficacy of this folk remedy for reducing or eliminating all effects of motion sickness, such as nausea, dizziness. Clinical trials also found ginger to be effective for relieving flatulence, relieving chronic pain and for acting as a natural antihistamine and decongestant. Scientists found that the active compounds in ginger, gingerols and shogaols, neutralize stomach acids, tone muscles of the digestive tract and enhances digestive secretions. This explains why it is helpful with nausea and flatulence. More surprisingly, it was found to dilate constricted bronchial tubes, which explains its role as an antihistamine and decongestant.

They also found ginger to reduce inflammation and to lower prostaglandins, which are part of the body's natural pain causing compounds. Topical application of ginger oil in neutral carrier oil is as effective as commercial muscle rubs for muscle strains and arthritis pains.

Ginger can be obtained in pill form as a standardized extract but it is just as easy to use the fresh root, sliced or grated into soups, salads or meals, enjoyed as a crystallized candy treat or imbibed as a tea or ginger ale. Be aware that many commercial ginger ales do not have much, if any, ginger in them so these are not useful for herbal supplementation.

Ginger has been found to be very safe for many ailments, including nausea from pregnancy. However, always talk with the doctor before attempting herbal supplementation. People with gallstones and those with bleeding disorders need to be careful as ginger stimulates bile flow, which can cause a gallbladder attack and it reduces the stickiness of blood platelets, which can increase bleeding times.

Black Seed

– Maryam O. Funmilayo

Names of black seed: The botanical name for black seed is Nigella Sativa. In English, it is known as nutmeg flower, fennel flower, or black sesame. In Arabic, it is known as haba al-baraka, seed of blessing. In Urdu, it is known as Kalonji. It is called Shuneiz in Persian.

Traditional uses of black seed: The black seed herb has been used by millions of people in Asia, Middle East, and Africa to support their health. In Egyptian, Indian, and Middle Eastern cuisines, it is used specifically as a spice. Traditionally, the black seed has been used for a variety of conditions, such as respiratory health, stomach and intestinal health, kidney and liver function, circulatory and immune system support, analgesic, anti-inflammatory, and anti-allergic reactions. It has also been used as an anti-oxidant against cancerous and viral health problems. Most importantly, it is widely known in the Muslim world because in Islam, it is regarded as one of the greatest forms of healing medicine available. It is narrated that Prophet Muhammad, salla llahu alayhe was salam, said:

"Hold on to the use of the black seed for in it is healing for all diseases except death."
(Sahih Bukhari: Volume 7, Book 71, Number 52)

Black seed in modern day medicine: Various research studies have been conducted on humans and non-human subjects, especially on the latter. These studies have taken place in research facilities such as the U.S. National Institute of Health (NIH), and the Anderson Cancer Center in Houston, Texas. During the research, natural compounds were extracted from black seed for potential anticancer properties. Though research is ongoing, some of their results have shown some very positive benefits of black seed as well as its oil, on skin and organ diseases.

In conclusion, I personally believe in the benefits of black seed because of the statement of our Prophet Muhammad, salla llahu alayhe was salam. As Muslims, we are blessed to have herbs, foods, and drinks alike, mentioned to us in the Qur'an and Ahadith. Hence, it comes to me as no surprise when the 21st century contemporary researchers are attesting to the huge benefits of these specific foods that are fully endorsed in Islam. Allaahu Akbar! Allaah is Great!

Cardamom (Habbahan)

– Sabah Negash

Cardamom is one of the oldest spices in the world. It is also a common spice used widely in many Middle Eastern and Indian dishes. It can also be found in Nordic dishes like the Finnish sweet bread, pulla or the Scandinavian bread, Julekake. It has a strong, fragrant aroma and warm, slightly sweet and spicy taste to it. It is a relative of the ginger. While the Cardamom plant resembles the ginger plant, it is the seeds of the cardamom plant that is used.

Cardamom originates from India where it is known as elattari. It is used as a respiratory tonic, circulatory stimulant, and adrenal tonic in Ayurvedic medicine. Ayurveda is a very old form of traditional medicine native to India, which means "the complete knowledge for long life". In Sanskrit, the word, Ayurveda, is broken into two words, ayus, meaning "longevity", and veda, meaning, "related to knowledge" or "science."

Cardamom is one of many key ingredients in sweet and savory Indian dishes. It is used with other spices like ginger, coriander seeds, black pepper, and cumin to make curry spices. It can also be used to spice up teas, coffees, ice cream, and sweets. Dried Cardamom seeds can be used crushed or whole. I like to use whole seeds when I make curry dishes but will often crush up a few pods when I make warm, spicy teas especially during cold/flu season. It is an excellent tea for colds and runny noses.

Tips:

- Cardamom is best stored in pod form because once the seeds are exposed or ground they quickly lose their flavor.
- Pods will keep for around a year if stored in an airtight container in a cool, dark place.
- When cooking the seeds, bruise them with the back of a knife or grind with other spices before frying.
- 10 pods equal 1½ teaspoons of ground cardamom.

Bibliography:

The Herb Bible: A Complete Guide to Growing and Using Herbs, Jennie Harding, Fall River Press, NY, 2005, pg 190.

Herbal Remedies: Visual Reference Guides, Andrew Chevallier, Metro Books, NY, 2010, pg 122.

Coriander (Cilantro)

– Saara A. Ali

"I love this chutney. It's fantastic! I can't get enough of it!" cried out Reem as she ladled a second spoonful onto the pakoras on her plate. "I'm sorry Sadia, I don't mean to be rude but I can't stand the taste of the chutney," exclaimed Jessica looking at me with an apologetic face. "What on earth did you put in it to make it taste so awful?"

As we sat there in my living room having our girls' evening I couldn't help but laugh to see the totally opposite reaction from my two friends. Their reactions to the presence of fresh coriander (cilantro) in the chutney were the same as many who have tasted this herb. Responses from total dislike to complete love and every shade in between are common. So what is Coriander?

Coriander is a plant known by its botanical/scientific name as Coriandrum sativum. It is used both as an herb and a spice. It's used primarily in cooking but is known to have medical application as well. From the fresh plant's leaves, stems, and roots to its fruits, almost every part of the coriander plant is used in cuisines of varying countries and cultures around the world.

The leaves and stems of the fresh coriander plant (also commonly referred to as Cilantro) are deep green in color and are used as an ingredient in marinades for meats, and in curries during cooking and for garnishing. The roots of the coriander are also used in cooking. The round shape fruits of the coriander plant when dried appear brownish yellow in color and are considered a spice and are used in pickling. When ground it is used in baking and curries. A little clarification is needed about names. The leaves of the coriander plant are sold fresh in markets and are referred to as Cilantro (which is a Spanish word) in the USA and as Fresh Coriander or Chinese Parsley in Europe and the United Kingdom. Whilst different names are used they all refer to the same plant. Another herb with a name similar to Cilantro is the herb called Culantro. Although the two plants are related they have totally different appearances, Culantro is less commonly available and it is known to have a very strong pungency. When Coriander (sometimes Coriander Seeds or Ground Coriander) is used in recipes, it typically refers to the spice made from the coriander fruit that has been dried and left whole.

So what's the practical meaning of knowing all these names? When you read a recipe and see "fresh coriander" or "cilantro" it requires the use of the fresh leaves of the coriander plant. When you see "coriander" or "coriander seeds" in a recipe, it refers to the coriander spice, found whole or ground in markets. ⇨

Coriander spice is described as having a nutty, lemon flavor. It is a distinctive, tangy fresh flavor. The dried whole coriander or coriander seeds is similar in flavor. The fresh coriander or cilantro on the other hand have a pungent, somewhat lemon taste and appears in cuisines in places such as Mexico and other Central American countries, India, South Asia, Thailand, Middle East and Mediterranean countries, and China. While fresh coriander can be found in use in Caribbean cooking, it is the culantro that is mostly commonly used as an ingredient in marinating meats. While most people like the taste of fresh coriander, some also dislike it. People from areas where fresh coriander is not commonly used have described its flavor as 'soapy.'

Coriander seeds, available whole or ground, are used primarily as a flavoring agent in the food industry or as spice in homes in breads, fish, meats, sauces, soups, confections, and when ground, is used as the base in much spice mixes (curries and masalas) in Indian and South Asian cuisines. Sometimes, seeds are used as a flavoring agent to improve taste in the preparation of medicines. Fresh leaves are especially popular where the plant is produced locally for use as a seasoning in curries, soups and stews. As a medicinal plant, coriander has been used as an antispasmodic, carminative and stimulant. Chinese herbal medicine includes the use of coriander for measles, stomachache, nausea, hernia, and as a tonic. The essential oil of the coriander herb is used in perfumes, soaps, and other cosmetics.

Bibliography:

C. Ramcharan, 1999. "Culantro: A much utilized, little understood herb." p. 506–509. In: Perspectives on new crops and new uses J. Janick (ed.). Accessed May 11, 2011, http://www.hort.purdue.edu/newcrop/proceedings1999/v4-506.html#medicinal

Gernot Katzer's Spice Pages. Accessed May 11, 2011, http://www.uni-graz.at/~katzer/engl/Cori_sat.html.

Olive Oil

– Sabah Negash

Olive Oil is known throughout the Mediterranean region and around the world for its health benefits, as well as its flavor in cooking. Olive Oil is used widely in foods, hair and skin products. It is grown widely in the Mediterranean region but also is cultivated throughout the world. Olive oil is made from the crushing and subsequent pressing of olives. The fact that olives are rich in oil is reflected in the botanical name of the olive tree, "olea europaea," as oleas means oil in Latin.

Here are few things you should know about Olive Oil.

1. The Olive is mentioned in the Qur'an, as being a "blessed tree."

"Allah is the Light of the heavens and the earth. The Parable of His Light is as if there were a Niche and within it a Lamp: the Lamp enclosed in Glass: the glass as it were a brilliant star: Lit from a blessed Tree, an olive, neither of the east nor of the west, whose oil is well-nigh luminous, though fire scarce touched it: Light upon Light! Allah doth guide whom He will to His Light: Allah doth set forth Parables for men: and Allah doth know all things." (Holy Qur'an Sura 24: Ayah 35)

2. The Prophet (pbuh) mentioned the health benefits of the olive and advised the Sahabas to use it.

Sayyed Al-Ansari narrates that the Prophet (pbuh) said,
"Eat the olive oil and massage it over your bodies since it is a holy (mubarak) tree." (Tirmizi, Ibn Maja)

Alqama Bin Amir narrates that Prophet (pbuh) said,
"There is olive oil for you, eat it, massage over your body, since it is effective in Heamorrhoids (Piles)." (Ibn Al-Jawzi, Zanbi)

Aqba Bin Amir narrates that the Prophet (pbuh) stated,
"You have the olive oil from this Holy (mubarak) tree, treat yourself with this, since it cures the Anal fissure (Basoor)."

Khalid Bin Saad narrates,
"I came to Madinah with Ghalib Bin Al Jabr. Ghalib became ill during the journey. Ibn Abi Ateeq came to see him and told a narration from Aisha (RA) that the Prophet (pbuh) told about the cure in Kalonji. We crushed a few seeds of Kalonji and mixed it with olive oil and dropped in both nostrils, after which Ghalib became healthy." (Ibn Maja, Bukhari) ⇨

Abu Hurairah (RA) narrates that the Prophet (pbuh) stated,
"Eat the olive oil and apply it (locally), since there is cure for seventy diseases in it, one of them is Leprosy." (Abu Naim)

Zaid Bin Arqam narrates
"We have been directed by the Prophet (pbuh) that we should treat the Pleurisy with Qust-e-Behri (Qust Sheerin) and olive oil." (Tirmizi, sanadeAhmed, Ibn Maja)

3. Olive oil promotes cleaner arteries and a healthy heart due to its richness in antioxidants and "good fats". It also helps balance good and bad cholesterol.

4. Food fried in Olive Oil retains more nutritional value than if fried in other types of food oils.

5. Olive Oil is excellent for healthy hair and skin.

6. A healthy diet including Olive Oil instead of other food oils is found to reduce the chances of developing certain cancers and cardiovascular diseases.

7. Olive Oil helps in the digestive process and is known to relieve constipation.

8. One main health benefit of olive oil is richness in antioxidants. Vitamin E is an active antioxidant present, which helps in fighting free radicals that damage the skin.

9. Olive oil health benefits also include some relief to people suffering from various ailments like asthma, arteriosclerosis, diabetes, stomach problems, rheumatoid arthritis, osteoarthritis, etc.

10. Olive Oil can be used in cooking and baking. It is a healthier alternative to other food oils and butter.

11. Olive oil is the only oil in the world, which has variety of natural flavors, and no two flavors are the same!

Learn more about the history and health properties of Olive Oil at these sites.

1) http://www.oliveoilsource.com/page/history-olive

2) http://tanbourit.org/olive_faq.htm

3) http://www.health-benefits-of-olive-oil.com/facts-about-olive-oil.html

5) http://www.oliveoilsyria.com/facts.htm

6) http://www.islamicvoice.com/february.2000/medicine.htm#ZAI

7) http://www.buzzle.com/articles/olive-oil-nutrition-facts.html

8) http://www.oliveoilsyria.com/history.htm

"What You Should Know About Olive Oil": Healthy food article: Previously published at Muslim American Girls Magazine online Mar/April 2010 Issue.

Honey

– Amina Malik and Balqees Mohammed

Linguistically, we have come to think of sweet things whenever hearing the word 'honey' uttered. It has even developed such a sensation of sweetness that it has become a word of endearment to call a loved one 'honey'. This holds true for the Arabic language as well as English, perhaps also other languages as well.

In the Qur'an, there is a whole chapter called "An-Nahl" (The Bees), in which these two verses are contained: "And your Lord inspired the bees, saying: "Take you habitations in the mountains and in the trees and in what they erect. "Then, eat of all fruits, and follow the ways of your Lord made easy (for you)." There comes forth from their bellies, a drink of varying color wherein is healing for men. Verily, in this is indeed a sign for people who think." (ch. 16, v. 68-69).

Concerning the truth of Prophet Mohammed (peace and blessings be upon him), we have these verses in the Qur'an, direct communication from Allah telling us of his reliable quality: "Your companion (Muhammad) has neither gone astray nor has erred. Nor does he speak of (his own) desire." (ch. 53, vs. 2-3); and: "Indeed in the Messenger of Allah (Muhammad) you have a good example to follow for him who hopes for (the Meeting with) Allah and the Last Day, and remembers Allah much." (ch. 33, v. 21) As a historical testimony to the truthfulness of Prophet Mohammed (peace and blessings be upon him), even those of his own tribe and countrymen who refused to accept the message of Islam as it was initially preached to them, confirmed his truthfulness, for he was known among his contemporaries as "the truthful one" and "the honest one".

The Prophet Mohammed (peace and blessings be upon him) also often recommended honey as a treatment for many ailments and disorders. The prophet (peace and blessings be upon him) has said: "There is no disease that Allah has created, except that He also has created its treatment."

Concerning precise treatment procedures or methods of cure, the prophet (peace and blessings be upon him) said: "Healing is in three things: A gulp of honey, cupping, and branding with fire (cauterizing)." But I forbid my followers to use (cauterization) branding with fire." In another instance concerning treating a stomach ailment with honey, the prophet (peace and blessings be upon him) repeatedly admonished a man complaining to him of his brother's stomach ailment to feed his brother honey, until finally, after several tries, the brother's stomach ailment was indeed cured.

Although Muslims need no such evidence to prove to them the truth of the sayings and directives of the Prophet (peace and blessings be upon him), still modern medical science is proving his words powerfully true. Honey has been proven to be a useful antimicrobial agent with potential for treating a variety of ailments, such as diabetic ulcers, applying honey as a topical treatment when conventional topical antibiotics are not possible due to their detrimental effects on such patients. Some studies have even shown that topical usage of honey in treatment of open wounds and burns reduces odors, swelling and scarring. It can even be useful in avoiding a dressing to stick to a healing wound, preventing further wound and damage to the skin as a wound needs to remain covered in the healing process. Even for the Jews, who are quite strict most generally in many of their eating codes concerning kosher foods, accept it as a pure food for intake, even though it is produced by a flying insect, which is considered a non-kosher creature. For the Jews, all products of all non-kosher animals are simply not kosher, or more simply put, not permissible for consumption. Except for the honey of bees, that is.

Taken orally, honey is an excellent agent to help treat consistent coughs, respiratory conditions, and ailments of the gastro-intestinal tract. However, it is not advisable to give honey to infants under one year of age, seeing as how their digestive tract is not yet developed enough to combat or handle the natural presence of botulinum endospores, which exist in honey.

The natural ingredients found in honey act as antioxidants, which are important catalytic features promoting anti-aging as well as a natural cancer fighter. In general, the darker the honey, the higher is the concentration of these antioxidants. Although honey is still in the investigative stage medically concerning cancer treatment, many first-hand witness reports are circulating telling the world of personal stories of the curing effects that honey has had on individual cases of various types of cancers. In addition, many manufacturers of beauty products and moisturizing creams have discovered the healing and anti-aging properties of honey, to the extent of its inclusion in many mass-produced products now available in the markets on a wide scale. Even many popular resort spas have learned the beautification properties of honey, so they include honey as a major and oft-used ingredient in many of their treatments available to their customers.

Honey is well known to be a rich source of carbohydrates, with a high concentration of sugars, having a glycemic index ranging from 31 to 78, depending upon the variety. It is a great energy booster for anyone, in particular athletes in training and competition. Even so, it is also an excellent agent in the fight against obesity, and is included in many widely accepted and proven weight loss programs. ⇨

Honey has been known perhaps since the age of mankind, for the practice of beekeeping and the harvesting of honey dates back to at least 700 B.C., if not earlier. It has been known to be an excellent preserver, for it was used in the embalming of personalities from ancient times, namely Alexander the Great.

It is also known as a miracle food, for it is perhaps the only food that never goes bad. Archeological teams discovered jars of honey dating back at least 2000 years in some of the Egyptian tombs, and when they were opened, they not only appeared and smelled as fresh as if they were packed yesterday, but they tasted fine as well. It is amazing that bacteria cannot grow in honey, because frankly, bacteria loves and feeds on sugar. However, the chemical composition, which is unique only to honey, is such that the environment of low water content combined with high acidic level, creating a low pH, makes it unfavorable for bacteria or other microorganisms to grow. Hence, its naturally good quality lending it as a good embalming agent, as well as a general preservation agent, such as in beautification for skin treatments. In addition to all of this, honey is the only food which includes all substances necessary to the sustainment of life, as it contains enzymes, vitamins, minerals and water. It has also been associated with improving brain function, as well as a proven immune system booster.

An interesting and inspiring quote comes from Royden Brown, a leading pioneer in the promotion of the benefits of bee pollen and honey: "Unique among all God's creatures, only the honeybee improves the environment and preys not on any other species."

Verily, there is indeed a sign for people who think in the fact that a healing comes forth from the excretion of the bellies of the bees.

Sources:

www.searchtruth.com (for hadith & Qur'an references); http://www.honey.com
http://www.benefits-of-honey.com; http://en.wikipedia.org/wiki/Honey

Cooking Tips and Healthy Eating Articles

Food For Thought
Sabah Negash

"Verily Allah has prescribed proficiency in all things. Thus, if you kill, kill well; and if you slaughter, slaughter well. Let each one of you sharpen his blade and let him spare suffering to the animal he slaughters." [Muslim]

I love tuna. It is amazing how some foods can trigger a long forgotten but treasured memory. We were very healthy eaters growing up. Not because we children wanted to be, but because for the most part, my mother was very conscious of the way we ate. She made sure we ate our FRESH fruits and vegetables with the occasional treat. Junk food was such a rarity for us. But that is not the memory I want to share with you. For a long time my family were vegetarians. No meat at all. Not by our choice or even my step-dad's choice. It was my mother who decided for all of us that meat would not enter the house. Now, we had not always been vegetarians. There had been a time when we ate beef, lamb, goat (rarely), and chicken. But then came along that one fateful day, the day that ended all the fried chicken, spaghetti with meat sauce, and beef tacos in our house.

One day, my step-dad decided to slaughter a chicken himself. Where we lived at the time, there were very few Muslims; in fact, there was only one other Muslim family that lived near us. Naturally, there were no halal butcher shops in our city or cities within 50 miles of our home. We usually had to drive to Los Angeles, some one hundred miles away, during our visits to my Grandma's house. So, Dad decided he'd do it himself. Having watched other Muslims slaughter an animal, he was very confident he knew what he was doing. He bought a live chicken from a nearby farm. He laid the chicken down, turned its head to the east, said "Bismillah", and cut the chicken's neck.

According to Islamic tradition, the animal should be hung upside down to let all the blood drain from its body. So, after about 15 -20 minutes, he returned to find the chicken still alive and flapping. Shocked, he took the animal down and he tried cutting the neck again. Back up went the bird and an hour later it was still flapping frantically like a chicken with its head still fully attached. By this time, my mother walked out to see my step-dad sawing away at the chicken's head as it flapped for dear life. I remember the expression on her face. It was a mixture of shock, horror, disgust and remorse. The poor chicken finally succumbed to the – for lack of a better word – torture, after some four or more hours. My mom shook her head at him and decided the chicken was no longer fit to eat or could even be considered 'halal'. From that day on, she declared we were vegetarians. I think guilt led my step-dad to agree with her. ➡

Section II – Herbs, Cooking Tips, and Healthy Eating Articles

159

Because of that incident, the only sources of protein we ate for years were beans and fish. My step-dad later found out that the knife he had used to slaughter the chicken was not sharp enough to cut through to the jugular veins. Years later, after hands on training with a few brothers, he sort of became a pro in his own right.

Tuna, as I was saying, was a staple meat in our family, growing up. My mother found very creative ways for it to come alive for us. She made tuna tacos, Potuna casserole, tuna croquets, tuna fried rice and more. However, she was famous for her tuna tacos! Even today, people ask us to make tuna tacos the way my mother did. My mother eventually went back to eating meat but after about ten years! http://fortyhadith.iiu.edu.my/hadith17.htm

Fast!
Mahasin D. Shamsid-Deen

At our home, we have always made sure that the children are just as involved in the preparation of Ramadan as the adults. When each was young, they were 'responsible' for fixing the fast breaking tray for those in the family that were fasting. Each child is unique. My son, Sudan, believed that fasting caused great hunger. He would fix a tray of sandwiches large enough to be a meal in itself. He always included a piece of cake, bean pie or sweet roll if available, and extremely large glasses of water or other sweet drink.

My middle daughter, Haseena, even at the tender age of only five or six years of age, would fix a fast breaking tray that rivalled any Martha Stewart presentation. She would decorate the tray with doilies and fresh flowers, use fancy cups for water and tea, and cut up fruit and sweets to arrange decoratively on the tray. She would even 'de-seed' the dates for ease of consumption.

My youngest daughter, Tasneem, had the unique experience of preparing for a large group as both parents and older siblings were fasting when she was that age. So she would prepare and assist with a table of food, which was always – apparently – almost irresistible, no matter how simple, no doubt because of the amount. It was common to see a grape or two in her small hands waiting for sundown.

The morning Suhur was also a time of anticipation and wonder. When she was five years old, due to the age differences of the children in the family, Tasneem found herself the only one not fasting during Ramadan. She would wake up and sit on the steps observing the activity of the household, clearly wanting to be a larger part than just being offered some orange juice.

One morning, we noticed that she wasn't on the steps watching but was instead very, very busy. She seemed to be preparing to leave. She was completely dressed and was pulling a chair to the front closet to get her jacket. She then sat on the steps to put string in her tenny shoes. Naturally, we all were curious as to what she was doing, and more importantly why. So we quizzed, "Tasneem, what are you doing?" "I'm just like you, I'm just like you!" she exclaimed. "I'm going to fast. I want to fast today like you guys."

All of us were happy and told her okay. She then put on her shoes, opened the door and peered into the darkness sceptically. "Um, okay. I'm ready. Let's fast. I can fast!" At first we were confused, but then realized that in her vocabulary world 'fast' was not a denial of something, but rather a quick movement. So as not to embarrass her, my husband picked up his jacket and said, "Okay, I'll fast with you Tasneem. And, we'll have a little talk about the different meanings of the word 'fast' while we're out."

This recipe is a staple used by our family when Ramadan is in the winter. The good thing about this is that the quiche can also be baked the night before and simply reheated.

Healthy Eating: What to Avoid
Linda K. Jitmoud

Fifty years ago, it was still easy to feed our families healthy, nutritious food from the grocery stores. Some of the food was processed, but most was fresh.

Now we must go to a health food store or a farmers' market to find the healthy food that was once so readily available. Most of what is sold in the supermarkets has been changed by adding chemicals to enhance flavor, lengthen shelf life, or even improve the appearance of the food. When we eat the food with chemical enhancers and preservatives, most of us don't give it a second thought. But our bodies do respond with aches and pains, and the chemicals can add up over time and create serious health problems.

Every time I buy food for my family, I make sure to avoid certain ingredients. The first is MSG. These days many labels claim that no MSG has been added, but this additive may be listed as something innocent sounding, such as "natural flavors." Other names for MSG include "modified food starch", "yeast extract", and anything either "hydrolyzed" or "autolyzed."

Another key ingredient to avoid is high fructose corn syrup. This can be found in sodas but also in syrup or ketchup. Some manufacturers have begun removing this from their products.

Finally, artificial sweeteners should always be avoided. The most commonly used these days is aspartame, which can be found in a wide variety of products including breath mints, low fat yogurt, and basically anything labeled "sugar free." The possible effects of aspartame include migraines and fatigue. Some contend that use of aspartame can also lead to chronic illnesses affecting the nervous system.

Allah gave us food to eat: meat from the animals, and fruits and vegetables from the earth. But humans have increasingly altered the food, making it less healthy and much less beneficial. When we buy food for our family members, and ourselves we must be careful to read the labels and choose either fresh foods or those with the fewest ingredients, and we must be careful to avoid that which could be harmful.

Healthy Recipe Makeovers
Anisa Abeytia

Life is moving fast and we have so much information coming at us that making choices can become a major source of stress. We eat at least three times a day, so it's a question that comes up more than once a day. Now add in the question, "Am I eating healthily?" and you probably feel like planting yourself and photosynthesizing. We all should be concerned about our food choices. Our food choices directly affect our health, but how many of us make those choices based on taste and convenience? You see, the trick is to find recipes that are both convenient and healthy. As a nutritionist, I work with clients all the time to help them find out what that would look like for them and their family. When we find the eating system that works for us, we can maintain a health weight, feel happy, alive and vibrant, and avoid many of the common ailments of today.

Autism, autoimmune disorders, adult onset diabetes in children, Alzheimer's and chronic fatigue syndrome are all new diseases in our vernacular. Never before have we been plagued with so many non-communicable diseases. This rise in degenerative disease, especially the rise of Autism, leads Dr. Mary Megson (a leading U.S. pediatrician, perhaps best known in her research and discoveries of the relationship of vaccine ingredients to the onset of childhood autism) to assert that we have altered the human genome. These changes have much to do with the foods we eat and do not eat. The work of Weston A. Price greatly highlights this connection, as he was a pioneer in establishing the relationship between nutrition, dental health, and general physical health.

Harvard medical school professor, Dr. John Abramson, in his book *Overdosed America*, stated that the rates of cancer and heart disease were both reduced more through simple lifestyle changes, like diet, than medical intervention. Yet, most people look for a pill to solve their ills instead of looking at food choices. It is easier to pop a pill than to change your eating habits.

Most of the food choices people make are the types of diet missteps that are causing our epidemic of lifestyle diseases. They are diet fads that change more according to the commercial food industry than due to science. Recall when we were supposed to consume margarine instead of butter and it turned out that we were all better off consuming butter because margarine can cause heart disease, diabetes and cancer?

Saturated fat is not bad for us; it is the man-made hydrogenated oils that are causing the rise in degenerative disease. Most of the studies that conclude that saturated fat is bad used hydrogenated oils and not butter, lard or coconut oil. One animal study that did attempt to discredit the use of coconut oil had one group of rats consume coconut oil while the control group did not (they followed a low fat diet). The researchers went a step farther and injected the rats with high levels of cholesterol (as if that will happen in nature). At the end of the study, the control group was still fatter. Both Dr. Abramson and the former *New England Journal of Medicine* editor, Dr. Marcia Angel, assert, "Much of the scientific data today is manipulated". The Framingham Study that is most often cited as a reason for lowering cholesterol and fat actually showed that the higher the intake of cholesterol, the healthier the person was.

The intake of calories is not the issue in weight loss or gain; the issue is that people are consuming too many calories that are not nutritious, and not consuming enough of the right type of calories. Caloric restriction is not the "gold standard" of any healthy program. The food choices we make are what will determine our health or degeneration. It is more important to eat an abundance of healthy calories than it is to be a human calculator.

In these recipes, (*Harira, Lasagna, Brown Rice, Sage Sausage),* I have taken the principles of healthy eating as determined by various researchers, doctors and nutritionists and applied them to some popular dishes. I have made a number of changes to the original recipes to accomplish this.

These include:

- Replacing "unhealthy" cooking oils, like canola, corn and other vegetable oils with healthy oils, butter and coconut. Here I am talking about cooking oils; you cannot heat olive oil. Not only do these oils cause inflammation, they cause oxidation, all clinical markers for autoimmune disorders, cancer, type 2 diabetes and cancer.

- Replacing unhealthy cooking methods with healthy methods. Over cooking meat and vegetables make them very difficult to digest because all of the enzymes are "cooked" out. Most of the nutrients are also cooked out as well.

- Replacing white rice and pasta with brown rice and brown rice pasta. White pasta and rice are also inflammatory which is important to reduce in conditions like autoimmune conditions, which are the fourth largest cause of death after cancer, heart disease and strokes. White rice is also a substance high on the glycolic index and should be avoided by people suffering from hypoglycemia, Syndrome X and both types of diabetes.

- Adding in sea salt, sea weeds and astragalus to cooking water to make them extra nutritious. I have included them in many of my recipes.

- Cutting out the soda, black tea and coffee; they are diuretics. ⇨

- Saying "Bismillah", doing dikar/tasbih or dua during the preparation of food; and fortifying food with the blessings of Allah.

Sources

Angell, Marcia. *The Truth About the Drug Companies: How They Deceive Us and What to Do About It* (Random House: 2005).

Abramson, John. *Overdosed America: The Broken Promise of American Medicine* (HarperCollins: 2004)

Fallon, Sally. (2001) *Nourishing Traditions* (New Trends Publishing: Washington D.C.).

Megson, Mary. "All About Autism" Designs for Health Professional Resources. March 29, 2006

Price, Weston, A. *Nutrition and Physical Degeneration* 6th edition (Keats Pub: 2003).

More Healthy Cooking Tips
Anisa Abeytia

1. *Deep Fried Foods*

The trick to deep fried foods is not to fry them at all. Most people fry them in vegetable oil that is not meant to be fried and is already rancid when purchased anyway. The result: a plate of DNA-altering grease balls which will leave you feeling heavy and lethargic. Instead, brush the dough or pastry with melted butter or coconut oil and then bake. They will be crisp and healthy. If you must deep-fry, use only virgin, organic, unrefined coconut oil. If the oil smokes, it is too hot and rancid. Also, do not reuse oil, and change the oil a few times if you are making large batches.

The only exception is the "special dough" made for samosa. You can use spring roll wrappers with this method.

2. *The English Fry-Up*

In England, as well as Canada and America, eggs, sausage and toast is a popular way to start the day. It is not a bad breakfast and is rich in protein and fats that can help you keep full for longer and provide the brain and body with very important nutrients. The problems begin when the proteins become damaged because of over cooking; the oil becomes rancid because of heat, or the correct oil is not used for frying; and when the bread is white. Additional problems arise when the meat and eggs are non-organic, because they are full of hormones and antibiotics. Today, many butchers offer meat that may not be organic, but do not have hormones or antibiotics in them, so make sure you ask. The commercially available sausage is also full of chemicals like nitrate salt, used as a preservative. Sausage can be prepared at home quite easily and then stored in the freezer. Omega-3 eggs are available and should be substituted for other types of eggs. When you fry them (in butter or coconut oil), do not over-cook, or you will kill all the healthy proteins and oils. The best way to eat eggs is sunny side up or "soft" boiled. As for the toast, choose wholegrain bread. Another variation is to add in beans, but that is a bit overkill. Some people do not do well with a high protein diet and it is not good to eat the same thing three times a week or more.

Eat Right According to the Qur'an and Sunnah
Maryam O. Funmilayo

Truly, Islam is a complete and comprehensive way of life. As Muslims, we are fortunate to have guidelines that serve as reminders to us as we go about our daily activities. From harvesting our produce directly from our family farms, to enjoying the dinnertime, and relishing the vegetables we harvested from our own sweat, practicing how to eat and drink right cannot be underestimated. For us to enjoy and earn the full rewards, sticking to the Qur'an and Sunnah is surely the way to go.

Thus, the goal of this very short treatise is to remind us to eat and drink right as Muslims. The outline below includes everything that will be mentioned. Hopefully, we will take up the challenge and get into the gear of developing healthy eating and drinking habits, inshaAllah.

Outline:

- BMI: What does it stand for?
- Case Scenario I, lifestyle, and discussion
- Case Scenario II, lifestyle, and discussion
- Comparison between both cases
- Islamic Etiquettes of Eating

So, what does BMI stand for?

BMI stands for Body Mass Index. It is a number calculated using your height and eight. BMI can be used as a screening tool to identify potential health problems.

BMI = Weight (in pounds) divided by height in inches (squared), and multiplied by a conversion factor of 703. For example, if one's weight = 150 lbs, and height = 5'5" (65"), then the calculation will be: $[150 \div (65)^2]$ x 703 = 24.96. Thus, 24.96 falls on the border of the normal weight range.

BMI Categories:

Underweight = <18.5

Normal weight = 18.5-24.9

Overweight = 25-29.9

Obesity = BMI of 30 or greater

Case Scenario one:

Name: Jenna

Height: 5'7"

Weight: 428lbs.

Age: 54 years

Marital Status: Married for 35years; blessed with 3 daughters

Occupation: A former business entrepreneur

BMI: 67, morbidly obese

Lifestyle:

Housebound because of her weight.

Has not seen the 2nd floor of her home in two years.

High blood pressure, high cholesterol, diabetes.

Breathing problems due to sleep apnea.

Lack of good hygiene.

Lack of marital intimacy.

Spirituality compromised due to lack of energy.

Overall health is failing.

Discussion:

This sister is being affected by an overall lack of quality of life because of her morbid obesity. We see that her conditions include diabetes, high cholesterol, and high blood pressure, which are directly related to her weight. Her sleep apnea occurs because every thirty minutes, her breathing stops. We also see that her spirituality has been seriously affected because of the inability to perform simple acts, such as wudhu or taking a shower.

Case scenario two:

Name: Ainul

Height: 5' 6"

Weight: 85 lbs

Age: 18

Marital Status: Single ⇨

Occupation: College student

BMI: 14

Lifestyle:

Obsessed with thinness.

Constantly assesses herself in front of the mirror.

Views herself as overweight.

Exercises one hour everyday.

Diet: 800 calories/day

She suffers from both amenorrhea and anorexia.

Her spirituality is also affected.

Discussion:

She has a history of collapsing and losing consciousness because of her anorexia.

Her family is concerned about her body weight. Medical help is sought on her behalf.

With her extremely low body weight, she is at risk of dehydration, heart failure, digestive problems, weak muscles, and fatigue.

Comparison of Jenna and Ainul below:

Jenna	Ainul
Morbidly obese	Anorexic
Immobility	Faints often
Lack of energy	Lack of energy
Unhealthy	Unhealthy

Islamic Etiquette of Eating:

- Know what you are eating. Read food labels, call food companies if a name looks strange or unheard of. Know the difference between halal and kosher.

- Always wash your hands before eating.

- Say "Bismillah". Aisha, RA, said,
"If any of you partakes of food, then let him say bismillah, and if he forgets, then let him say, "in the name of Allah, in the beginning and in the end." {Hadith Tirmithi}

- Eat with your right hands, as right-handedness was the practice of the Prophet (SAW) in all his actions.

- Eat what is near to you.

- Three-fingered selecting: using the tips of the index, middle, and thumb fingers.

- Not eating while reclining. The Prophet, sallallahu alayhe wassalam said,

  "As for me, I do not eat while in a posture of reclining." {Bukhari}

- Eating a fallen piece of food

- Not eating too much. Allah commands us in the Qur'an ch. 7 vs. 31, to eat and drink freely but also warns us not to be excessive. For indeed, Allah does not love those who are excessive.

- Show gratitude to Allah after eating

- Wash hands after eating

Islamic advice and reminder:

The Prophet Muhammad, sallallahu alayhe wassalam, said,
"The son of Adam fills no container with anything worse and more evil than his stomach. Sufficient for him are a few morsels of food to keep him on his feet. Beyond this, let him divide his stomach into 3 parts: 1/3 for his food, 1/3 for his drink, and 1/3 for air." (Hadith Tirmithi)

A Spiritual Recipe - Food for a Sustainable Heart
Uzma Mirza

Beyond the white fence, along the horizon, a hue flutters to transform those that gaze upon it into a glimmer of light. There, at the edge of the bound blue sea, is the rising sun where the honeybee breathes and the Ababeel sleeps. It is a resplendent Recipe, that glee glue glorifying only His Names, as the ingredients of His water; the drink and food, to nourish all hearts. A recipe, whose ingredients are already painted on the universe's canvas for all eyes to see, as the pen dips into its inkpot to write the Divine Names, and reflect that same Recipe like an insatiable ink. A recipe reminder that surrounds the Art of the natural world, which we subtly see through signs of our Creator's presence, yet absence, that can forgive and allow us to step off this stage and only eat food with ingredients, that is a healthy recipe, building us into goodly trees, saying goodly words. Spiritual food for the heart is the Recipe of my Divine Architect, whose created ingredients I see as 'surround sound'- a spiritual Recipe with universal insight, like the music of the reed, swaying gently in the cool dawn breeze.

A universe with a score on a staff designed to heal, to teach and to nourish the thirsty and hungry to health. The universe is composed of a tonal palette of ingredients that score to reflect the Recipe. The Recipe that continuously reminds: from the rustling of the leaf and the swaying of trees, to the flight of the hummingbird, the weaving of the tailor bird and the sweet diverse nectar of the honey bee; from the dive of the Swift to the power of the elephant; in each ingredient exists the Divine Recipe, as a quiet score, an *ode to joy* from Beethoven's melodious drawer. To know one's heart that yearns, to be satiated of its thirst and hunger, amidst the carnal that seeks matter in only a need and only wasteful synergy. To be souls at rest and return home is the quest; and not let loose an untamed self of only matter that becomes deaf, blind and unable to reason the Recipe for a sustainable heart; to be where one's thirst and hunger will only satiate the moments passed until the next windy anxiety, unharnessed, wants to be.

As I imagine a walk to Shangri La, traversing along a winding narrow path, over mountains, vast oceans and erupted volcano aftermaths, the ingredients of the place emerge, to remind me of that Holy Grace towards which I race. In each place like a cupboard, a shelf, and a rusty sea, I sail to see that delight lit in every step, where a Divine Decree lies as the healthy Recipe to be. I see ingredients, which are in me, that can heal this delicate soul free. It is a palette not black and white but a harmonious staff of variegated colors, scoring a delight even in adversity. A healthy array of ingredients I see, compose the natural world scored amongst diverse hues, languages, beings and moving oppositions, that know knowing knowledge in light of each other, is not to hate.

So what is this recipe, entailing such endearing, yet foreshadowing ingredients like remnants of the future; ingredients that can shower us with resplendency and unstain our hearts ware?

There, the ingredients are reflected in our body, our motion, our speech, and in our action and reaction; ingredients composed to constitute balance in our lives and give us peace. It is to read this Recipe made aware, if we look, and created as a sign stewarding sustainability in the worlds amongst all things in both the East and the West is the question to be, or not to be? Here, there and everywhere lie the ingredients of one's self and the Recipe is not lost.

It is not a paradise lost except for those who have forgotten their self's role limited to an institutionalized stage of actors and actresses. It is not the glee club that will rock and roll your soul, but the 4th score that will give a heart to your drum role by stopping, pausing, and breathing your heart at its core, to remove that pollution and satiate a thirsty and hungry heart. Before me now, and in front of me, lies this Recipe in the signs of the natural world that can sear souls smoothly to a heavenly abode to breathe. A little balance, a color of green, a pinch of love and the reading of these ingredients is all it takes. A Divine Will designing ingredients to make a recipe for action and release, to unshackle this matters fare, to be able to read verses, that fill the spiritual appetite and harness the carnal self; to feel that real shade beneath these wings we have lay to waste, as our Recipe is being lost within our heart's taste. A sound heart is like wings that can help us soar high, even amongst rocky and bare peaks and shower our soul with the ingredients of our resplendent Recipe-food for our soul to know. The ingredients must be composed from the nature of things, like light amidst darkness, where photons shimmer between the rustling of an olive with a chlorophyll green; where compassion composed carefully is love, patience and forbearance; where a cold stream emerges on a hot and arid day; or the shade of a prolific tree heavy laden with time hovers to evaporate the heat that burns you; when an oasis is not a mirage in a desertscape; and when water rains and gray clouds stain the earth with their unpolluted heavy vapor, as they release their shower upon a barren and dry land giving life to a prolific green foliage growth.

Alas! Reflect to seek these ingredients, like an instrument of hide and seek, for they can only be found if one searches and confronts trials and tribulations by harnessing that carnal self. Knowing when to sit and when to voice are part of this Recipe to speak, as the circle must be first squared for the heart to see, heal and be blessed with Mercy. ⇨

So now flows from these fingers a harmony to compose a symphonic Recipe that nourishes the heart and tame its matter on a staff that is digestible; not meek, but gentle, assertive and articulate; with goodly words as the ingredients of the tongue, the body, and the mind. It is harnessing herds of unruly stains on the mirror of one self-from whose polish emerges the Recipe to know that Divine Light to produce a food that will nourish the spiritual self like a green tree and tame the carnal matter with a self truly free!

So I read the Recipe to find the ingredients, as food for thought, for my phototropic heart beat to *Tock*, silently, each cool morning *Fajr* dawn sought.

The History of Muslim Cookbooks
Dr. Freda Shamma

There are more cookbooks in Arabic from before 1400 A.D. than in the rest of the world's languages put together. The Muslims in those days were unique in writing recipes down, compiling them into cookbooks and cooking from them. The preparation and eating of food was such a pleasure that even the heads of state, the caliphs, enjoyed cooking and talking about it. In one story related by a Muslim historian of the 900's, Al Masuddi, the Caliph and his brother, the wazir (Prime Minister), and Head of Security forces were enjoying each other's company. The topic was food and each was bragging that his cooking was the best. To find out who was really the best, they brought in an unsuspecting man from the streets and asked him to judge which dish was the tastiest. The man recognized who the audience was, but pretended ignorance and proceeded to taste the various dishes. Of the one prepared by the Caliph, he said he had never tasted anything better. Of the Caliph's brother's, he said the dish was so similar in quality it must have been cooked by a relative of the first cook. He also praised the wazir's dish, but said of the last dish, it was the worst thing he had ever tasted. The Caliph was so amused by the man's answers that he awarded him a great sum of money and invited him to join them on a regular basis.

Not only cooks and historians and caliphs concerned themselves with food, but Muslim medical writers often discussed recipes in their books as well. One famous physician, Ibn Jazla, compiled an encyclopedia of substances that were considered to have medical benefits, and included several dozen recipes as well. In the fourteenth century, his recipes were translated into Latin and later into German.

The oldest surviving Muslim cookbook, *Kitab al Tabikh (Book of Dishes),* was compiled in the tenth century by a scribe named ibn Sayyar al Warraq from the recipe collections of eight and ninth century caliphs and members of their courts. Charles Perry has translated it into English under the title of *A Baghdad Cookery Book.*

Here is one recipe from *A Baghdad Cookery Book,* written down sometime between 900-1000 A.D. I don't recommend letting your children try it. The recipes usually included the term "throw" as in "throw it on the ground" before rolling out pastry, and "throw some rice in the pot"!

Shurba, A Meat Dish

The way to make it is to cut up fat meat into medium size pieces. Then melt fresh tail fat, discard the cracklings from it, throw the meat in the fat and stir it until it browns. Then throw on warm water to cover, a little salt, a handful of peeled chickpeas, slender sticks of cinnamon and bunches of dry dill leaves.

When the meat is done, throw on dry coriander, ginger and finely ground pepper. Increase the water which is in the pot with warm water, and kindle the fire under it so that it comes to a full boil. Then take the dill from the pot. Take cleaned rice which has been washed several times and throw the necessary amount in the pot, and leave it on the fire until the rice is done.

Then cut the fire from under it and sprinkle it with cumin and cinnamon, both finely ground. Wipe its sides with a clean cloth and leave it on the fire awhile, then take it up. Do not leave it until the rice has thickened strongly. If you want, put in some meatballs of pounded meat.

Ma'moul
Balqees Mohammed

Ma'moul: A traditional date-filled cookie/pastry of the middle-east.

The word *Ma'moul* is an Arabic term, meaning literally and simply something that is made, but more precise, and in particular concerning this individual food item, it means something made by hand. This is quite a fitting name for this article of food, for in every stage of the game, the hands play an important role in the formation and completion of it.

The *ma'moul* itself is a type of cookie or sweet pastry, but as you read along in the recipe and directions of making it, you will come to understand how the hands play such an important role in the making of it, to the extent of it having become named as such. Of course, in all that we do, even in our typing and writing, our hands are an important tool which we most generally cannot do without, and without which much of our work would be impeded, if possible at all.

However, with this food item, you will notice how it is the hands that form, shape, and create this pastry from the beginning till serving, for there is no rolling or pressing or cutting involved. In other words, no other tools in addition to the hands other than the mold used to make the decorative design on the top, the pan or sheet on which they are placed for baking, and the oven for the heat of the baking process.

After the preparation of the dough, the pastry itself is formed into a tightly pressed round ball in the hand, with the date mix filling firmly placed in the middle. It is then placed into a mold of sorts, which is carved out in the center with a decorative design. Once pressed firmly into the mold to acquire the design on one side, the side of the ball facing out is pressed firmly to attain the design into the pressed dough, as well as to attain a flat edge for the bottom. The finally pressed pastry is then taken out (either through a push-button type fixture in the mold, or simply knocked upside down on the counter a few times to get it out), placed flat side down on the pre-greased pan or cookie sheet. Once full, it is then placed in the pre-heated oven for baking until it begins to become slightly golden around the edges.

The pastry is extremely hot inside once baked, so not a good idea to bite into one until thoroughly cooled. They are not easy or comfortable to eat hot, as are chocolate chip cookies. Also, if you desire to have the extra addition of powdered sugar for the top, do not do this until they have cooled completely, or the sugar will simply dissolve into the cookie, with no remnants of it remaining as a decorative covering. Once the cookies/pastries are cooled, they will be a bit hard or crunchy. If you want them to become softer and chewier for serving, place them into a tight-closing plastic or glass container, one with a tight fitting lid such as Tupperware. However, to ensure that they do not become excessively soggy in the process, make sure that you do not do this until they have cooled properly. These pastries will usually keep good for up to one month. After that, the baked pastry becomes rather crumbly.

Ma'moul is an excellent and nutritious fill for easy on-the-go snacks and wonderful for serving with coffee or tea any time.

A Traditional Egyptian Meal
Judith Nelson Eldawy

In the Mediterranean style, the main Egyptian meal of the day is lunch. This can be served anywhere from 3pm to 6pm, with the earlier hours being more usual. Dinner is late and light and breakfast is on arising; though it will be a sit down meal only on holidays or other days off. The same things are enjoyed for both breakfast and dinner. Traditional items include but are not limited to: falafel, fava beans (fuul), sliced tomatoes and cucumbers, French fries, mashed potatoes or fried eggplant sandwiches, a variety of cheeses (rumi-sliced Parmesan, Gouda, soft cheeses like telega and istanbouli, farmers cheeses like areesh and mish, or processed cheese triangles like President or Laughing Cow), eggs, yogurt, breads, and everything imaginable pickled.

Proper meal time etiquette calls for one to rip off a small piece of bread and use it to dip out selected items, or wrap the ripped off piece around falafel, veggies or cheeses. Eat only with the right hand, as the left is considered unclean.

Bread and rice are the main staples in the Egyptian diet. Riots have started over the cost of rice or lack of bread. These two important items are government subsidized and price controlled. Government stores, called tamween, are located in every village and neighborhood and sell price controlled rice, corn oil, sugar and other staples.

Aish beladi (village bread) - huge pita like rounds of coarse flour - is sold for a shilling or 20 rounds for 1 Egyptian pound (about 17 cents in US dollars). The local bakeries selling the government subsidized bread bake only this and will control how much is sold to any one person. Some days they only allow an individual to buy a half pound worth of bread.

Private bakeries operate and sell different types of breads, cookies and pastries. There are several styles of pita rounds, distinguished by the type of flour used. Yeast based breads are made here; the most popular style being aish feeno, which is a cross between a hot dog bun and a sub roll. You get 5 pieces for 1 Egyptian pound.

Many Egyptian women start preparing lunch directly after breakfast so that the kids can eat it when they return from school. Many of the public schools do not have cafeterias attached so the kids bring sandwiches from home and get biscuits (cookies) and chips from vendors at or outside the school. The prevailing attitude, at least in Delta Egyptian families, is that sandwiches are no more than snacks.

The basis of most Egyptian cooking is a well prepared stock. This can be made from any poultry (chicken, duck, goose, pigeon, etc.) or meat (beef-cow or water buffalo, goat, lamb, camel, etc.). Once the stock is finished, the meat is fished out of the broth and quickly browned in butter, ghee or sumna-a popular butter-like granular substance. The broth is then added to a basic tomato sauce to flavor the vegetable of the day and used to make a pasta based soup called lissan asfour, which means bird's tongue, named so for the pasta's shape. Orzo is what this pasta is called in English. The stock may also be used to cook mashi, which can be any number of rice stuffed vegetables (cabbage, zucchini, small white eggplant or peppers).

Rice is so important to Arab cuisine that many Egyptians believe if there is no rice at the meal, they did not eat. They also believe if one cannot cook rice well, one cannot cook.

Food combinations are also very important. I learned that while rice is indeed important, the regular rice made with vermicelli pieces called sharayah or just fried rice grains is only served with chicken or meat dishes. If you have fish, then you must have an onion or tomato rice, which can only be eaten with fish.

All pasta is called macaroni and if you have kofta, grilled or baked meatballs; then you must have elbow macaroni. If you have leftovers, they can be eaten with aish beladi or other pita breads.

Guests and hospitality to guests is hugely important to Egyptians. The amount of dishes served and the effort that went into making the dishes is a reflection of how honored the guest is. Mashi-a labor intensive effort involving rice stuffed vegetables is often a company dish. So is macaroni béchamel, having both meat and chicken offered or making stuffed pigeons.

Dinners are finished off with fresh fruit and tea. Sweet desserts are rarely served after a typical Egyptian meal. They are most often enjoyed as a late dinner or breakfast, as a snack or served when special guests visit.

Editor's Note: You can make your own Traditional Egyptian Meal for your family by creating the recipes Judy Eldawy contributed to this cookbook: *Egyptian Eggplant Pickles, Chicken Stock, Lissan Asfour Soup, Basic Tomato Sauce, Rice - Egyptian style,* and *Salad - Egyptian style.*

No Pork for Me
Linda D. Delgado

I had a vague awareness that becoming a Muslim would require some changes to my eating habits and cooking. Like many reverts, I did not study Islam at great length before making my decision. I didn't know any Muslims to discuss the practical matters of cooking and eating. My two Saudi police officer house guests didn't get into discussing cooking with me and they returned home within weeks of my reversion. I understood I'd have to give up eating pork and drinking alcohol. I didn't drink alcoholic beverages so no problem was my thought. Basically I just jumped right in going pell-mell down the path of Islam, and clueless.

The first niggling clue that I might be in over my head was when I was reading an email posted in a sister egroup on the Internet. The discussion was about how meat should be slaughtered. The more I read the more uncomfortable I became. The no pork rule was just the tip of the iceberg!

I mean…well you see I was 52 years old when I reverted so I had eaten maybe hundreds of pork chops, ham with pinto beans and cornbread, slices of pork roast, hmmm bacon…. and bar-b-q pork spare ribs. And I have to say this…it all tasted good! I know it is abhorrent to Muslims born into Muslim families and never having eaten pork, but to millions of reverts… we grew up eating pork cooked many ways and we did enjoy this haram food. We just didn't know about it being haram.

Okay…like I said… I thought I was dealing just fine with the 'no pork issue', but I was reading another email discussion about reading labels on food products to see if they included any pork products or byproducts. Ka-Jam… nope… I hadn't even thought of doing this.

And then the big No-No that was like being slammed into a wall. I learned I wasn't supposed to be eating any meat with blood in it and the meat had to be slaughtered in a special way on top of that. Yikes. I loved beef: fried, broiled, baked, in stews, as bar-b-que, whatever and my favorite was a medium rare steak….with the meat slightly pink and juices running out of it! Now eating meat in this way was a really huge life-long practice and to think about never enjoying a medium rare steak or roast again was some serious stuff to consider. Was my fledgling faith strong enough to deal with all of these food challenges?

Realizing that I would have to buy only halal meat (at least for me) was something I was concerned about. I could not picture how meat was slaughtered and worried about health codes and sanitation etc. ⇨

I went to an Arab market (owned by Muslims) across the street from the masjid I was going to and learned that halal meat was sold there. I looked at the meat. E-U it looked funny and not so appetizing to me. I bought some anyways to try it out and hoping I would not end up a vegetarian. I really don't like vegetables that much... at least not cooked veggies.

Now I have to be perfectly honest with you all. I had read emails in this sisters' egroup about halal meat having a better taste...so I was really hoping this was really the skinny and this would compensate for my loss of eating a rare cooked steak. Let me tell you this. There is a difference in how the halal slaughtered meat tastes and how non-halal slaughtered meat tastes. I did not prefer the halal slaughtered meat. It wasn't a bad taste... but it was different and something I was not used to. I said a prayer after those first few bites asking Allah to help me grow to like halal meat!

I thought at this point that I had overcome the worst and could live with my new dietary requirements. That was until I read the email about marshmallows, marshmallow crème, and Jell-O. Gads! I thought. There went my marshmallow crème floating on top of hot chocolate and globed onto Ritz crackers. All GONE! And I wanted to cry just thinking about the loss of my lime Jell-O with pear halves on a leaf of cold, crisp lettuce...and what about giving up one of my favorites: strawberry Jell-O with sliced bananas! Was I a happy camper? No I was not. Later, much later, I learned about halal substitutes.

Until I reverted to Islam I had never bothered to read the labels on food products I purchased. Reading labels made going to the store to shop a whole new experience and required at minimum another hour of my time.

But this is just the beginning of the challenges I faced and possibly other Muslim reverts face. Contrary to what some Muslims think, not all new sister-reverts end up getting married to a Muslim man and then getting help with many of these types of challenges from his extended family members. Some reverts are just too old to want to get married again after being widowed or divorced.

Back then and today I have non-Muslim family members of diverse ages living in my home and depending on me to cook (or supervise) and serve their favorite foods. Did I try to gain their agreement and willingness to go along with my new cooking and eating lifestyle? Did I make changes only for me and continue cooking the same for my family as I did before my reversion?

We had one of those family sit-down talks and came up with a compromise. I would not cook any pork meat or have pork in the house. They could eat pork elsewhere if they chose. I would continue cooking for them the foods they enjoyed while monitoring my own cooking and food intake for myself.

SERVING UP FAITH

But …the "No Pork for Me" food saga didn't end here….

My husband and I were empty nesters for 12 years before my granddaughter was born and became an immediate member of our household. During those years we enjoyed dining out three to four times a week at a very diverse selection of restaurants. Once I reverted I was challenged to find items on menus that would be halal for me to eat. While eating out so much we had honed to a fine science our ordering methodology and habit of sharing what we ordered with each other. This would have to change and it was difficult at first as my hubby was not pleased with all the 'restrictions' he felt there were to our old ways of dining out and enjoying a leisurely meal together without us having to do anything but relax and enjoy the food and conversation.

As my husband wasn't big on eating meat this was a blessing from Allah and made things so much easier. After a few stumbles and some minor irritations we both experienced, as time went on, it became easier and finally routine when selecting from menus foods we both could enjoy and share. We found that eating at higher-end restaurants provided opportunities to talk to wait staff and even cooks about menu items. Most chefs enjoy talking about how they prepare food.

The good news is that by the time my first Ramadan arrived I was ready and no longer floundering and ignorant.

It took some time and effort and most of all prayer for patience. Overcoming my ignorance and then learning and understanding the importance of halal meat and food preparation to being a practicing Muslim was one of the biggest challenges I faced as a Muslim revert. Thanks be to Allah I succeeded with His help and the patience of my family.

Section III – Inspirational and Faith-based Stories

Lifestory
Abdul Rahman Nazir El Dosoky Mojahed

To describe me, you can call me "a chip off the old block". My father learned the Qur'an by heart and received a religious education since his early years. While in Al-Azhar secondary school, he joined a Sufi order, after which he led a mystical lifestyle. He served in the 1973 war as a Reserve Officer, and his life was saved in every situation in which it was endangered. After his military career he reluctantly sought marriage at the advice of a learned Sheikh. However, he could not afford marriage costs, nor had he a desire for marriage given his spiritual devotion and religious dedication. The sheikh of his order pressed him to get married so that he would "beget good offspring" according to this sheikh. So, fellow members of the order arranged for his marriage to a daughter of one of the dignitaries who used to take the order members in when holding their spiritual sessions in Damietta city. My father responded to his fellow members of the order and proposed to the girl.

Thus, the marriage became a reality. Married life was not initially what my father expected, but extended family members and friends helped them settle differences that inevitably arose.

Soon, the pressures of life overtook the marriage and my father had to cater to our needs. A timely opportunity for bettering himself came as he was offered a job to teach Arabic in Saudi Arabia. With the need for such a position, he soon traveled to meet the challenge.

As a matter of fact, his travel, albeit temporary, was a curse to me and my older brother. In my father's presence, there was a kind of balance in our life. He was kind, tolerant, helpful, and merciful, unlike my mother who was offensive, aggressive and irritable. My father traveled to Saudi Arabia when I was about six years old and came back when I was about ten years old. This period was fairly critical and demanding. I think those four years were the worst years in my life.

I resembled my father in many things, but I was quite alienated from my mother. When my father was away, my mother took charge of us. Naturally aggressive and offensive, she was too harsh and her feeling of responsibility and the necessity to act as both a mother and father made her even harsher. I hated her as a mother and a woman so much so that I hated all women.

As most of my teachers in the primary school were women, I had difficulties in education which were exacerbated by my inability to learn by heart the things I did not understand. I could be educated neither by dictation nor memorization.

My learning problems were further complicated by attending a religious school, namely Al-Azhar Primary School in Damietta. I was enrolled in such a school for my father was an official in Al-Azhar Directorate in Damietta and my mother was a clerk in this school. As you may know, religious education in Al-Azhar is also based on dictation and memorization. So my education in the primary school was quite a suffering.

However, I excelled at the mundane subjects, which were not based on dictation or memorization. But I was a bad student in all subjects involving dictation and memorization, especially, of course, the Qur'an and religious subjects. As a child of a local directorate official and a school clerk, I was supposed to excel at all subjects, but this was not the case. So the teachers of religious subjects were angry with me and they would not personally punish me, but they would punish me by proxy, that is to say they would tell my mother to punish me in front of my colleagues who included girls.

My hate for all women, which was based in my hurt from my own mother, was only reinforced because of the way I was treated by my teacher.

Consequently, I had terrible complexes about things that usually led to my degradation and humiliation. In addition to my hate for women, a rejection or hatred of the Qur'an and Hadith also sadly grew within me, because they were associated with the women who taught them to me, and they were associated with dictation and rote memorization. I even maintained a rejection of any type of affection and anything feminine or related to the religion.

Fortunately, my father came back from Saudi Arabia. His return from travel was a turning point in my life, and coincided with my enrolment in the preparatory school and the onset of puberty. I learned true Islam from him and got to know how to put it in practice by following his good example of tolerance, mercy and general consideration of others.

I developed interest in religion and I would discuss religious issues with my father who used to talk to me as a man, rather than a child or teenager. He passed on to me much knowledge I most likely would not have attained elsewhere.

Another turning point in my life was my father's early death. He was only fifty four years old. His death caused me considerable hardship for we had many things in common. On his death, I lost my father and best friend. I could not communicate with others, including fellow members of my family, any longer. I felt lonely and thought about committing suicide.

There was always an atmosphere of misunderstanding and disagreement at home, necessitating a third party to mediate. No disagreement could be settled in direct terms. Sometimes, I would leave my family's house for some time. I would live with my grandmother or any other close relative.

However, the divine providence took due care of me. Several months prior to my father's death, when I was only fifteen years old, in my first year in the secondary school, I fell in love with a girl whom I saw as the solace which Providence sent me. I loved her so much that seeing her once would give me enough relief until I next saw her. She continued to be the best thing in my life throughout my secondary school education.

I cannot imagine how I could keep alive without this girl. In the stated period, I lived for her. Love for her gave me immunity against all of my problems and difficulties. Several years later, when I graduated and had a suitable job opportunity, I went to propose to her but in vain. I found out that she had got married several years earlier. Again, I was left alone.

Just as my father, this girl unintentionally played a very important role in my life. My father put an end to my hate for religion and substituted such hate with deep love that yielded great fruit soon. Similarly, this girl put an end to my hate for women and substituted it with affection, respect, reverence, and sometimes sympathy. She was truly a very important player in my life.

I could not be a good Muslim if I continued to bear grudges against women or any group of people. Thank God, as He brought my father back to rehabilitate me in terms of religion, He also sent me this girl to unconsciously reform me in terms of woman's input in this life. I owed her so much love and reverence that I had to change my vision of women by and large. She did me a great favor without even knowing about it.

It was at this point that I began to understand the reason of my existence.

I saw my father in a strange dream several years after his death. I see him quite frequently in my dreams, telling me of something which comes to be soon afterwards. This dream took me by surprise because I was convinced that I was a bad boy and unlikely to be a good man one day given the estrangement and alienation I suffered. I thought that this might have been just a dream. While I paid little attention to it, I kept it in mind until I had a stranger dream where I met Prophet Muhammad who seemed to have been waiting for me. I greeted and embraced him and then we kept talking about something seemingly important but I could not identify it at the time. The Prophet Muhammad seemed happy for meeting and talking to me though I used to see myself as a contemptible sinner.

Though this dream was strange enough, it gave me much relief and a lot of hope for reformation and eagerness for putting in practice the exchange I had with Prophet Muhammad seeing the prophesy coming true. At the time, I suspected that I might have been of some human value, with potential of being a good man or influential Muslim personality.

Having passed through one difficulty after another, from being accepted initially into the faculty of languages at the University of Al-Azhar, to eventually passing exams after a second round, it became evident that it was in my destiny to have an important role in the honorable work of calling others to Islam.

Subsequently, I resumed my study in the faculty in peace throughout the first year. But the second year marked another important turning point in my life. It was this very year that witnessed the above prophesies beginning to come true. This year gave birth to my first book which had a story not less strange than my overall life story.

As the University pays little attention to this department, to the point that many of the teachers are in fact volunteers or very low paid, we were assigned a young female teacher who tried to force her opinions and warped interpretation of a modernized Islam upon us. Due to her own personal tragedies and experiences, she had developed a hatred of men as I had developed of women, and she had developed a rejection of everything traditional of Islam, calling for a modernized reformation of Islam and its teachings. This awakened in me the realization of the need for some literature to prove the truth of traditional Islamic teachings, by which I developed the idea of composing a book giving solid Islamic proofs of the high value of women in Islam. Hence, the birth of my first book.

Another important occasion in my life that required a book to be authored was doing my military service immediately after my graduation. I joined the Department of Military Intelligence (DMI) where I undertook the translation of intelligence reporting. I was very annoyed at the intelligence reporting I was translating but I could do nothing in response. So I developed a plan of a book on Jihad in Islam while I was doing my military service. Once I left the army, I set about the book. It is now under publication and due to be on the market in the foreseen future.

Consequently, I hope to go ahead with my writings about the true essence of Islam in order to lend the misguided people a hand and guide them to the way of Allah just as He rightly guided me when I urgently needed assistance.

My Own Miracle of Islam
Balqees Mohammed

At the date of writing this note of memories, I've been a Muslim for over 30 years. Seeing as how I became a Muslim at the tender age of somewhere between 18-19, it doesn't take a highly specialized mathematician to figure out that the majority of my life has been spent as a Muslim.

Although I admittedly accepted Islam based upon my feeling of faith rather than true firm knowledge, I've never once felt that I made the wrong decision. I came into Islam at a time in world history when there was very little literature in English language about the religion, other than the common everyday propaganda against it (in the news, etc.), or the very slim explanatory paper handouts (produced mainly by world-class Islamic organizations such as WAMY-the World Assembly of Muslim Youth) which mentioned only the limited facts about the basic tenets of Islam, i.e. the five pillars. There was no other more deep explanatory literature available such as we have today, the growing numbers of first-hand stories of conversion/reversion, or more in-depth explanations of the meanings of the basic tenets of the religion. Even when I did become a Muslim, there was still a very limited amount of literature available for me to learn my newly accepted religion from. In fact, the only books of which I had immediate access to were a copy of the English translation of the meaning of the Quran, and a similar translation of the collection of Sahih Bukhari, one of the most reputed collections of hadith available to Muslims to this date. It was this collection of hadith, which was a gift given me by a brother upon my initial conversion, along with the Quran, which I treasure until this day, and from which I dutifully learned most of the more detailed aspects of the religion.

Soon after my conversion (in fact, essentially within a day), I married the same man who initially introduced me to the religion months earlier. However, as my marriage and conversion were both within such close timing with one another, many people tend to mistakenly suppose that I became a Muslim because of the marriage, or to facilitate the marriage. It was in fact the opposite, for it was my becoming a Muslim that truly facilitated the marriage, and in fact I made it clear from the very beginning, that I would never change my religion for any one person, but for my own self, only if I felt it right for me.

My husband was keen that I learn the specifics of the prayer initially, for he is a firm believer that all else is based upon that one aspect of a Muslim's life and practice. And, he has supported me in the years after that initial acceptance, always there for me when I've needed guidance and had many questions, and making sure that I had the right accompaniment of proper female companionship as well, to help guide me and shape me into the Muslim that I have developed today.

Within two years after my conversion, my husband finished his education for which he was sent to the U.S. from his homeland of Saudi Arabia, and we moved to K.S.A. after his graduation from University in the States. We have lived in Saudi ever since, going back to the U.S. for occasional visits to my birth family, which I love immensely.

As I have hailed from a typical western protestant family, I had to adopt several practices after I became a Muslim, two of these things in particular, the style of dress and manner of eating. I mean, there are many Muslims around the world who are not particular about following the dress code of donning the hijab (for the ladies), but I opted to adopt it from day one, for I knew that this was a command that Allah has presented to us in His Book (the Quran), and so never once questioned the authority of this directive. The same thing can be said for the dietary rulings, particularly concerning that of ingesting any pork products or derivatives, and alcohol. I immediately adopted all of these practices, without question.

After moving to Saudi Arabia, I've learned a whole new world of cooking and eating as compared to what I had been exposed to earlier in the U.S. First things first-when I first moved to K.S.A., there were no modern shopping malls or western-style grocery stores as are prevalent today. There were what is known more commonly as corner markets at which most dried goods and paper goods could be purchased, but canned foods and many other pre-prepared or factory processed foods were basically unknown in this country back then, in the early 1980's. All foods were (and for the most part still are) prepared with the freshest ingredients: from the spices to the oils, from the meats to the vegetables, even the breads baked fresh in open deep-pit type ovens fueled with wood fires. Our meats are taken from the freshest and most recently butchered animal, to the point that we many times butcher our own animal, have it chopped or sectioned at the butcher shop, ready for packaging in our own deep freezers for our own usage throughout the month.

As I look back now upon my transition into Islam and into the life of the Arabs, I recall that many times it was not so easy, but I was fortunate to have a supporting family along the way, which helped me immensely. However, if I had not been patient to persevere through some of the trials which I've encountered along this path, I would not have learned many of the jewels of knowledge which I've been privileged to have learn.

Not meaning to sound boastful of myself or my accomplishments, I will tell you that I have long ago become bi-lingual, having learned the Arabic language quite well since my earlier years in Arabia. As I've learned the language, it has made it easier on me to not only communicate with my in-laws and other people in the community here, but it has enabled me to understand the many lectures by well-versed Islamic scholars, as well as understanding the books of the source of knowledge for Islam: i.e. the Quran and the various volumes of hadith recording the sayings and history of the Prophet (PBUH) and his companions (ARA). Why, I've learned the language well enough to realize some mistakes made in the original (first edition) translation of the Sahih Al-Bukhari books. Much is lost, confused, or even sometimes sadly distorted in translation of any literature into another, and the books of Islam are definitely not an exception to this. In fact, the books of Islam are perhaps the strongest example of this point. It is because of this realization that I always try to impress upon any Muslim who has come into Islam from another life, another religion, and another language, to try their best to learn Arabic, so that they are not at a loss, depending upon translations to guide them, or at the very least, to find dependable and reliable sources of translated material, and perhaps dependable persons to accompany those translations by helping to explain things along the way.

In speaking of my learning the language of Arabic, I must not ignore the fact that this is indeed a miracle in and of itself. As I said earlier, I come from a basically protestant family. Everyone in my family essentially believes in God, although not all worship or recognized Him in the same way. But we did all recognize that there is a God, and we were taught (in both the home as well as the church) to pray to Him, particularly in times of need. I've always been a firm believer in the power of prayer, even long before I became a Muslim. In fact, it was a prayer that I offered to God, which eventually led me to finally becoming a Muslim, after I sought His divine guidance in my quest.

When I first moved to Saudi Arabia, I had a command of a very limited vocabulary of words, and could put together only the most primitive and simplest sentences, things like asking for milk or diapers for my infant daughter, or other basic necessities of life to help get me by. When we moved to Saudi Arabia, my husband was a new college graduate, and immediately received his first official job appointment upon our return. For several reasons, we lived in the same house with his immediate family at that time, which consisted of his mother, father, aunt, and 3 brothers and 3 sisters who were all not yet married at that stage. They were of varying ages, ranging from my age at that time (approximately 20 by this time), down to about 7 years old. My husband's job took him out of town all week long, allowing him to return home only on weekends, many times shortened because of the long drive for him back home at the end of the week. It was an even shorter weekend because he was so tired from the traveling he had to do during the week, that he needed most of the weekend to simply rest up for the upcoming week of travel and work. Our infant daughter and I remained at home with his family, none of which knew any English other than basic vocabulary they learned in the mandatory classes of English at school.

In addition, at that time, there was no such thing as computers or internet in our lives, nor were there any additional satellite stations nor even a selection of English language video tapes. All I had for my English-language outlet and pleasure at that time were a few novels, magazines, and other books I had brought with me from the states, or a very aged English-language program (sometimes originating from the U.S., sometimes British) aired on the (one) Saudi national TV station, once daily. Programs that aired at that time were selections such as "Bonanza", "Little House on the Prairie", or something a bit more modern like "CHiPS"-most of which were already 15-20 years old at that time. I'm no TV addict, not then and not now, but for someone to find their self immediately in an environment in which no one speaks his native language, it is a relief at times to hear something spoken in the native language once in a while, whether on TV or radio or whatever.

My language (Arabic) was very broken and sparse, to say the least. Many times, it was difficult for most of the people to understand me, whenever I got up the nerve to speak up. I usually only spoke out of necessity, to express needing something around the house, or to ask my brother in law to bring me what I needed for my daughter in the line of milk or diapers. Other than that, I rarely even spoke. And I understood even less. I would always make a mental note of various words that I noticed as familiar, and save them for when my husband was around, so that I could ask him for a translation. I eventually built up my vocabulary in this manner. But I didn't understand the mechanics of the grammar to put things together into understandable and workable conversation. And I understood even less to get the accent flowing on my tongue.

It was not until I became flustered by my daughter's refusal to respond to me speaking English with her, to the extent that she would, as she was just beginning to learn to speak herself, respond to me (correctly, I must add) in Arabic, adding on the extra arrow through my heart that she didn't want anything to do with this English. That pushed me into literal nightmares. I woke up in crying sweats nightly from the worry that my own daughter (and whatever other offspring I may be blessed with, for I was at the time pregnant with her brother who followed her) would grow up into a fine young woman, but I wouldn't be able to communicate with her or understand her, nor she me. I had these dreams, or actual nightmares, that we (the ladies of the family) would be ushering her down the aisle on her wedding day, dressed in the finest beautiful wedding gown, she surrounded by her grandmother and aunts, with me off to the side, because the two of us (myself and my daughter) did not know each other's language. I never once mentioned this dream to anyone. All I did was I cried my heart out to Allah on my prayer rug nightly, asking for help, asking for some interference, asking for a blessing of any kind, to relieve me from my fright that my daughter would grow up in this atmosphere and that we would not be able to communicate because of my block with the Arabic language.

One morning, after spending the previous night in prayer and crying about this situation and fright, I woke up as usual, but felt something different. It was as if a light was literally lit for me, and indeed it was. As I took my daughter downstairs, and proceeded to join the family for breakfast, I noticed something strangely different. They were speaking with one another, as usual, but what was different was how I heard them. At this time, the different conversations going on did not have that *foreign* sound to them that they previously had. As I took note of this, I also took note of the fact that I was picking up nearly every word now, and recognizing that I understood nearly every word being said. Strange, indeed, because only the night before, everything had still been so foreign to me. It was then that I thought to myself that I should try out my tongue, just an experiment, to see if it was the same as my ear, or the same as it was the night before. I mean, I could not possibly be any worse than I was previously. Nothing to lose, eh? So, I did it. I tried out my tongue. I think that perhaps I was more surprised than the family was, for I stopped almost immediately, before picking up to continue on. I can remember the jaws almost literally dropping, and all eyes suddenly glued on me now. Made me rather nervous, but I was so enthused with my new ability to accentuate the language and speak my heart, that the nerves were abated by the sheer excitement of the moment.

Although I still had (and still do to this day) much to learn about the language, I cannot deny that what took place was nothing less than a miracle of Allah answering my call and plea to open up my heart, my eyes, and my brain, to help me in my predicament of the language barrier, and to ensure that my children did not grow up with a vast gap of language difference between me and them. I learned the language well enough that I've been able to adopt the accent well enough to disguise to most I come in contact with the fact that I am not originally an Arab. I've even coached or tutored my children through their early years in the government school system here, which is basically an all-Arabic curriculum. As I said earlier-no real feat or accomplishment of my own to boast about, but rather a miracle from Allah, in that He so graciously granted me this blessing of understanding, insight, and ability, and relieved me of the hardship of worry that my children would grow up without me being able to properly communicate with them. They (my children) in turn have also been blessed to have learned English as they have grown into adulthood, and each proudly graduated from universities now, and in their own respective fields of work, using their skills in English to their fullest abilities.

This is not a story of simply my own conversion to Islam, nor meant to be a boast of any of my own accomplishments, but rather a story to remind all of the importance and value of prayer, and to realize that nothing in this life is too small or insignificant to bring to Allah in prayer. Even the smallest of things is truly worthy of bringing to Him in prayer, and a miracle can indeed befall any of us, if we are indeed so blessed to be the recipient of that blessing.

My Conversion Story
Linda K. Jitmoud

I tried to convert the first Muslim I met. At the time I was a junior in college and hoping to attend seminary after graduation. The first Muslim I met was an international student from Thailand who had come to the university to earn his M.A. He spoke about God and had good manners and I thought it was such a shame that he would go to hell because he wasn't a Christian, so I set out to convert him to Christianity.

My first step was to invite him to church. He came, and he brought a copy of the Qur'an with him. No one said anything, but I was so embarrassed. After the service we walked over to Pizza Hut and he began telling me a little about his faith. It was the first time I heard the word "Islam."

Over the next two years we saw each other often, and we each remained strong in our respective faiths. In May 1978 I graduated with my B.A. in Philosophy and Religion and he completed his M.A. in Social Science Education. I went on to seminary in Chicago. He remained in our college town to work on his Ed.S. degree. We kept in touch.

Attending seminary was a mixed experience for me. I made some great contacts with professors at the nearby University of Chicago, and studied Latin with a Polish priest who was very excited when John Paul II became pope. But I became disillusioned when my professors told us not to share certain theories with our future parishioners, and especially when I was reminded to "not question, just believe." After a semester, I left seminary and moved back home with my parents.

My baby sister, a wonderful surprise, had been born the previous May. I spent some time taking care of her and decided to watch her for signs of original sin. I found none. Later I took temporary secretarial jobs in various areas of St. Louis, my hometown, and began reading on the bus and during my lunch breaks. One day I bought a paperback translation of the Qur'an. My purpose was to read it and, using my religious knowledge, find the mistakes so I could prove to my Muslim friend that his religion was wrong.

So I started reading. I didn't find any mistakes, but I also didn't find anything that touched me until I came to this verse: "He it is Who created the heavens and the earth in Truth; In that day when He says Be! It is." (Surah 6.73) When I was a child attending Sunday School I had learned that when God created the world He said, "Let there be light," as reported in the opening verses of the Bible. After reading that verse, I began to think that maybe the God Muslims worshiped was the same God I had been worshiping all my life.

That fall I returned to the university to earn my M.A. in Philosophy and Religion. My Muslim friend was still there. I decided to study all religions and try to find where I belonged. To that end, I read the Bhagavad Gita. I also read the Bible, cover to cover, and examined the historical roots of beliefs about the Trinity and the divinity of Jesus. I studied Chinese religions and I attended worship services with students who were Baha'i. I also observed the Muslim prayer nearly every Friday and asked many questions of my friend and other Muslim students.

Many things about Islam appealed to me. By the summer of 1980 I was left with only one reservation, and that was the necessity of making ablutions before prayer. As someone who had grown up Protestant, it seemed to be an unnecessary requirement.

One hot July night I was sweaty and uncomfortable and couldn't fall asleep in my apartment. I read a little but sleep wouldn't come. So I decided to pray. I was lying there in my bed and I folded my hands, as I had always done, and started to talk to God when suddenly it hit me that I couldn't pray because I wasn't clean. I got up, made wu'du as best as I could, as I had been taught by one of my Muslim friends, and prayed. Then I went to my typewriter and wrote a long letter to my Lutheran pastor. In the letter I said that I would probably have to become a Muslim.

At 4:00 AM I was finished. It was Ramadan and I knew that my Muslim friend, along with two other Muslim men, were awake in the apartment they had rented. So I went there with the letter in hand. When I arrived they had just finished their morning meal and were praying. I waited. When they were ready I showed them the letter. They read it, became very excited, and took me to the bathroom and showed me how to make wu'du properly. Then we all sat down and one of them, a Muslim from Egypt, told me how to say shahadah. I tripped a little, but I said it.

Soon afterward I went back to my apartment and slept. Later that day, at around 2:00 PM, I woke up and wondered at what I had done. I took a walk around the university quadrangle and, when I was finished, decided I would give it a year. I could always change my mind, couldn't I? That was over 30 years ago.

My Voyage into Islam
Maryam O. Funmilayo

Have you ever heard of someone born as a Muslim into a Muslim family, revert back to Islam? If not, here is my story, for I am one of them. My journey into Islam is my own story, a strong part of my history that I will never forget.

To Allah belongs all glory and praise. He is the only one worthy of worship and He is the only one worthy of seeking help from. Each time I have a flashback of my journey into Islam, my eyes fill up with tears. My tear ducts become uncontrollable. Tears of both joy and sorrow; tears of fear and hope; tears from appreciation and gratitude to Allaah for giving me the chance to live extra few years on His earth before I breathe my last breath.

I came into this world in the United States by the grace of Allaah, when both my late parents (may Allaah have mercy on their souls), traveled many miles from Africa, to pursue their college and graduate studies. They were Muslims, alhamdulilaah, but not practicing. Hence, I was never exposed to the basic teachings of Islam during my early childhood years in the United States. We moved back to Nigeria when I was five years old. So, for the next thirteen years of my life, I was wandering in ignorance, oblivious of where I came from and why I was in existence.

I attended Catholic elementary and high schools. I knew many things about Catholicism and their ways of life, much more than what I knew about Islam. In fact, I did not know anything about Islam other than being Muslim because my parents were Muslims. In my elementary school, I took part in their religious rituals, joined the assembly choir to sing songs of praise from the hymn book, and also, ate the bread of life during the Holy Communion services.

Every day at 12 noon, when the school bell rang, we had to stop all what we were doing and recite the angelus prayer. In addition, I was not known in school by my Muslim name. Muslim names back then, were not in vogue. To the Christians in Nigeria, especially the Southern part of Nigeria where I grew up, Muslim names sounded unsophisticated. Muslims were looked down upon and regarded as illiterates. Being a Muslim in a Catholic school was not the usual norm. Many of my classmates knew me as "Kemi", which is the short form of my middle name, "Oluwakemi". "Oluwakemi" means, "God blesses me". The name "Kemi" is a name that is very common to both Muslims and Christians in Nigeria. So, many people just thought I was a Christian.

I vividly remembered one day when a visiting teacher came to my class. After introducing herself to us, and asking us our names, she went further to ask if there was any Muslim in the class. I did not know why she asked that question and I did not bother to ask her why. I reluctantly rose up my right hand. Most of my classmates were in total shock. They said there was no way I could be a Muslim because I did not look like one. So, how did Muslims look like? To my classmates, they looked uneducated, goofy, dirty, and poor. They also concluded that Muslims attended only the unfunded government public schools and not private schools. One big thing did intrigue me as a young, naïve, innocent Muslim girl in an orthodox Catholic elementary school. I noticed that the Catholic nuns dressed the same, in their long blue and white dresses, as well as their veils, which did not reveal their hair. Of course, I never understood why they dressed differently from the rest of the teachers. However, I had this inborn respect for them and always was in awe whenever I came across them in the hallways.

My experience in the Catholic high school was totally different. Once founded as a Catholic school for girls, suddenly got tagged as a "born again" school. It was in high school that my deen became an issue and Muslims were targeted with full force. Some of the born again girls had a big mission: to convert Muslim girls into born again Christians. I was one of the Muslim girls and there was a particular girl that made it her duty to visit my class every day, just to chat me up and ask me point blank questions about Islam. Unfortunately and sadly enough, I had no perfect response for her about Islam. The only answer I had for her intimidating questions was: I was Muslim because my parents were Muslims. It was so obvious to my high school colleagues that I knew absolutely nothing about my religion.

The born again era in the late eighties and early nineties were intense and overwhelming such that some of my Muslim friends got converted into Christianity. It started becoming the norm to see a Muslim girl whose parents were highly respected in the Muslim community, declare war against Islam. Such girls had the full support of their Christian friends and they were showered with lots of gifts and money. It was a scary situation. I began to live a double life. Though I performed my acts of worship, and fasted in the month of Ramadhan while I was living with my paternal aunt, my life was a different ball game every day in school. I joined them in singing songs of praise at the morning assembly, including their morning prayers. It was just impossible for me to opt out.

As Muslims, we have been promised in the Qur'an that after every hardship, there is relief and ease. Yes, I finally got relief from the "born-again" peer pressure after I was given admission into the university. Not that there was no born again pressure in the university. But the presence of the Muslim Students' Society alone, gave me a chance to breathe fresh air. It was at the university that my journey into learning the basic principles of Islam began.

It was there that I knew the definition of Islam: total submission to the will of Allaah, the Most Merciful and the Most Compassionate. It was there that my self esteem shifted from a below zero level to a high level. I felt so good inside out. I no longer felt intimidated. I felt the gush of confidence. I was thrilled to meet so many Muslim students in different fields. I always looked forward to attending the Friday services. Islamic programs became part and parcel of my daily life. The lifelong friendships I made helped me spiritually, socially, and academically.

I have lived in the United States for eleven years now, and I must admit that my faith in Allaah, and my deep quest for Islamic knowledge took place here. Yes, all praise is due to Allaah who blessed me with sincere friends back home, who took it upon themselves to teach me the basics of Islam. However, my faith grew more with understanding and contemplation since moving to the United States. I have met so many Muslims from all walks of life and from richly diverse cultures, and I have learned a lot from knowing other Muslims who do not hail from my native country. It is here, in the United States, that I knew the difference between cultural practices and Islamic practices. Back home, it was easy to mix and match both practices without knowledge. But here, we have many shuyookh readily accessible for us, to answer our questions. That alone is an asset. We can easily get Islamic knowledge on our finger tips by the grace of Allaah, and also through the power of the 21st century high technology.

My voyage into Islam has been a soul-searching life experience. Wherever one finds himself or herself, be it in a Muslim majority country or Muslim minority country, one should seize the opportunity and grasp the reins of knowledge. I am so blessed to be alive today and be able to call upon Allah's beautiful names. For He has truly guided me to the straight path when the many paths I had trodden in the past were full of thorns. Subhana Allah.

Conversion Story

Soumy Ana

Year 1991.

Highlight of the year: re-transplanting my faith.

I could not possibly choose anything but Islam.

Islam was in me, dormant, ready to come to the surface.

I was made to become a Muslim.

I have always hated alcohol in all its forms, even in the French cakes that often call for rum or liquors.

I detested all pork products, from "pates" to sausages.

I always wore a scarf although only on my shoulders or on my head outside in the cold winter.

I could not stand tight and revealing clothes even if I weighed 100 lbs when I converted and I did not have any infirmity.

I did not like dating. I was looking for the one person I could give everything.

My Catholic upbringing kept me away from stealing (very common for teenagers in France) or lying.

And, I prayed every day to God to show me the right way.

I may have been material for the convent if so guided early in life. I may have become a missionary if so directed.

I may have been more involved in Catholic life, but the problem was I was convinced Christianity was not the religion God wanted for me. I could not explain why; there was something in me, deep inside.

Maybe it was because I did not like the trinity and I was confused most of the time about whom I was supposed to pray to: Mary, Jesus or God? Maybe it was because I did not like the Catholic rituals with lighting the candles and kneeling before statues. Or, maybe again it was because the priests disgusted me with their plump bellies and their condescending ways. Maybe mostly it was because priests hated me because I had embarrassing question about the scriptures.

So, becoming Muslim was the easiest thing for me. It was the most natural thing that happened to me.

How did it happen?

Allah has always a way.

First of all, I must confess that one of my dreams was to fast during Lent. I envied the nuns for doing it, but I did not dare do it because of my parents who were completely opposed to it.

So, when I heard one of my sister's friends was fasting for Ramadan, I was very excited. I remember that day so clearly I can relive it in my head over and over again. My sister's friend was from Mali. He was married to a Christian but actually was Muslim. He tried hard to stay Muslim in a non-conveying environment and was often referred as being "different." Good for him! We were walking up the stairs of my University when my sister whispered in my ear, "Do not kiss him on the cheek." In France, we always kiss on the cheek to say hello. Not kissing someone is even an insult, so I was very surprised. She added quickly, "He is different…" "How is he different?" I asked my sister Dominique with an open heart. She looked embarrassed; she tried to avoid answering. "How is he different?" I insisted. She turned her eyes away. To be Muslim sounded like a dirty secret.

Then we said hello and I piped up to excuse myself, "I am not kissing your cheek because you are different." He looked at me very amused. Everybody looked embarrassed. I looked straight in his eyes, waiting for an explanation. His wife Christina looked upset; she added very quickly, "Bakar is fasting." Fasting! I had no idea he was Muslim and I had no idea what this religion was all about. But he was fasting. I knew it was for God, and I could not imagine a most beautiful gift one could give to God! That sounded incredible! Amazing! I clicked with him. I admired him right away. "Fasting?" I asked, "How do you fast? How long?" Christina interrupted, "We have to go." Bakar kept looking at me very amused and I just could not keep my eyes off him. Waww! He is fasting, I thought. This is so amazing. I wish I could do it too!

That was my first contact with Islam.

Bakar was a sweet Muslim, but every time I started asking him about his religion, people intervened and blocked out conversation. Maybe it was Allah's way to tell me I was not ready and I had to prepare myself for Islam slowly. Maybe it was a way Allah hungered me for Islam.

Whatever the reason, Allah knows everything and He knew that, a year later or so, I would have an occasion to fast.

I had met other Muslims through my sister still and I managed to ask how they did the fasting. So, I tried. And then, at the end of the Ramadan, I decided on my own to try to pray like Muslims do too. And when I did, I could not do it any otherwise, so I kept doing my *salat* without knowing the words or the exact *rakaas* or even what a *rakaa* was. I felt in my heart, without knowing much about Islam, that this was for me. That sounds

incredible, but my heart was at peace with Islam. That's all I needed. I did not feel
the way I was confused while being Catholic. I did not even know I was Muslim
a Muslim friend told me I did not need to revert, I was already a Muslim because I
everything they did. I just needed to learn how to do it properly.

So, becoming Muslim, in France, surrounded by French Muslims who shared the same
culture, was easy and natural for me. Despite the daily racism I faced in France, my faith
only became stronger and like a halo of peace.

But living in a foreign country now, surrounded by Muslims from different origins,
where being Muslim is not a threat to many, that is the hardest for me.

I left France because I did not want to cry every day anymore and I did not want to be
called "towel head" anymore, but sometimes I wonder if, by leaving France behind, I did
not leave also behind the most beautiful years of my Iman.

Hajj Year 2002 - Back to Islam

High points of the following year: my removal from the community and the deepening
of my faith.

All of us could tell a story of a renewed faith. All of us go up and down the hilly events
in our faith. To maintain our spiritual integrity, we have to be good climbers. We have to
pass over our mood swings, our disappointments, our anger, our desires, and our upsets.
It is like going up and down hills. That requires endurance and will power. Sometimes, we
do not have what it takes to go all the way to the summit, so we fall back until we gather
enough faith to go all the way up again. It happened to me. I am not the exception.

However, the most astonishing fact about going to the bottom, for me, was that it
happened at the period of the highlight of my faith: hajj.

I departed for hajj like millions of other Muslims that year.

Hajj is the hope in the heart of every living Muslim. No wonder, it is one of the pillars
of Islam. It is the promise of coming clean from sins. When we go to hajj, we go to the
birthplace of Islam. Every Muslim I know has only one dream -- one day, go to Mecca,
Saudi Arabia, for the yearly pilgrimage. And once again here, I was not the exception. I was
very excited about hajj. Yes, me. But that's where I was soon going to stop sharing feelings
with my community.

We arrived first in Madinah.

The journey to Madinah did not go smoothly. Instead of taking a plane to go there, we
got stuck somewhere a few miles from Jerusalem; however, we were not allowed to go to
Al Aqsa because of the Jewish occupation. We almost did not make it to Madinah, so we

for several days to Allah to allow us to finish our journey. The guides
re talking about getting the same reward as going to hajj even if we
e United States. Sometimes I wonder if maybe that would have been

ded in Saudi Arabia. Everybody loves Madinah. For me, the whole
e Prophet, the scent of Paradise, the calm respite of faith. In Madinah,
nd all day without feeling sleepy or wanting to be parted from the
Prophet's mosque. Madinah resembled the state of faith I was in before hajj; I felt home.

A week later, it was time for hajj.

Everybody fears Makkah, and for a reason. Makkah is the hardest place on earth for Muslims. I did not know that. I thought hajj would be the natural continuation of the path I was following. It would be heavens, a spiritual journey that would help propel me to another level of my faith. And it did the opposite. For me, it was a gut of hell that would engulf me for almost a year. During hajj, my heart soared and was crushed. My happiness was great but was trampled over every step of the way. I emerged bruised and deeply hurt from a voyage that was going to be the completion of my faith.

Who finally broke the last pieces of my heart? Who crushed it in the first place?

There were many candidates.

Maybe it was the women who pushed me back in the lines for Wudu over and over again. Maybe they did the most damage. I remember trying to get to this water for an hour and return to the tent defeated, tears in my eyes, and there I found other women who scorned me for not having prayed dawn prayer yet.

Maybe it was the woman who took my food portion, collected the cookie and gave it back to me without a word.

Maybe it was the older lady who yelled at me every time she saw me until I asked her why she yelled at me on sight. "You smile too much," she answered. "You laugh too loud." Was that a reason?

Maybe it was one of my roommates who could not speak a word of English after staying in the United States for forty years. She asked our third roommate why I did not speak Arabic. I told her I was busy learning other things. "I see…" she scorned, "too lazy."

Maybe it was the "Imam" who escorted us and yelled at us over and over again until I could not bear it anymore. "Sabr, brother, sabr. Please!" I had to tell him. I tried hard not to hate him.

Maybe it was these guardians of the mosques who begged and those guardians who insulted me because I had a small water full of Zamzam in my bag. Maybe it was the one

SERVING UP FAITH

who pushed us to the front row in mid salah to teach us to close the gaps.

Broken pieces of my heart they broke, one person at a time, one after the other.

Maybe it was the hotel manager who pretended not to hear me when I asked for new bulbs over and over for the very dark bathroom, or the server who refused me one glass of water, or the Malay couple who shouted at me when I smiled to them.

I felt frustrated to tears when I could not understand a gentle Imam explaining Islam in Arabic and I wanted so much someone to translate. I felt so excluded when even our group discussed in Arabic and I had no idea what was going on. I felt crushed when an Imam gave a Khutba in the next tent in English but they did not want me to join because it was not my tent. I felt moved around like a toy in a bathtub that is being emptied. It was with an overwhelming feeling of sadness, exhaustion and anger that I boarded the plane to leave Mecca.

And when I came back to the United States, I found the wudu women, and the Imam, and the guardians, and all the little persons who had broken my heart in debris during hajj, and I recognized them one by one. I knew that if I travelled with this person, what this person would do. Living among Muslims is one thing, but traveling among Muslims gives you an idea of what our community looks like from the inside. And I was not very happy about the insight. I thought over and over in my head about every step of our trip. I did not feel like living in this community. I could not stop thinking that if Islam was a great religion, people had to be great too. What was a religion worth if it did not reform people's hearts? Satan was really playing with my head.

I read somewhere that when hajj is done, the angels surround you and tap on your shoulder to congratulate you. I also heard that Satan stands right behind, ready to start hacking you. I guess that my faith at that time was at the top, so Allah wanted to try how strong it was. And it came through the door of a great disappointment.

So, when I returned from hajj, I curled around the new life that was growing in me and I decided to hold on to what was left there.

My husband would say, "It's Fajr, it's Fajr, you used to push us into the car to go to masjid," but I would feel like a nausea coming up just at the idea of being among other Muslims.

My husband would insist on saying, "I do not see any light in the middle of the night anymore. What has happened?" Surely the baby made me too tired, but I just felt like a hypocrite and I felt like my salahs were probably not accepted anymore because of this weed growing in my heart.

My husband would say, "Come to the khutba with me; you used to give lectures at the mosque," but I had work to finish. In fact, I just could not admit that I could not stand anyone speaking in Arabic anymore.

That's when I discovered these feelings in me that I knew would destroy me. I felt betrayed by my community. I kept wondering why Islam had such a great message when the message was not applied, not even in places where it mattered more than anywhere else. I did not feel I belonged anymore.

When Ramadan came, I finally went to masjid and on this first day of Ramadan Allah gave me my first child. Muslims whom I did not know cared about us came to visit me, while Muslims I expected to come visit us did not come at all. New people, new hopes. So, I looked at the guardians and at the Imams and at the people who had sewn the weeds in my heart and I decided that the weeds sometimes looked beautiful too. Any light in the darkness I was in was good. I started to take people in slowly without expectations. I grew new roots. Ibn Umar said that the Prophet said, *"For every action there is a period of enthusiasm/activity and for every period of enthusiasm/activity there is a period of rest/inactivity. So he whose period of rest/inactivity is in accordance with my Sunnah then he is rightly guided, but he whose period of rest accords with other than this, then he is destroyed"* (Ahmed)

I never stopped praying and I never stopped making duas and Allah did not take away the faith I had in my heart, but it took me nine months to forgive Muslims their shortcomings. It took me that long to appreciate people as people and not anymore people as the example of what our faith should be. Allah remind us in the Qur'an that we will all be tried, in our wealth, in our children, in our health and do not think you will not be tried because other people before you have been tried. That's the way Allah separates the hypocrites from the true believers.

At the end of the trial, I am confident that I passed the test, but how many around me are tried every day by our shortcomings? I am sure every one of us is at different levels. I am sure I am myself sometimes a trial for my brothers and sisters too. But I guess that's how Allah wills it.

As I look around my life and how it changed, and I think of myself as a garden. We have a house and we did not pay as much attention to our garden as we should have had. One side of the lawn is now full of dandelions. When I see the lawn, I think of what I went through. The dandelions may not be pretty to look at, but they are still flowers. I have a new appreciation for weeds. The gardener told us to kill the weeds in April and then plant new grass seeds in September, and next year, we will have a luxurious front yard. I like to think of myself that way. Underneath all the weeds, there is still a very good soil.

The weeds are like my memories of hajj. Maybe when each and every dandelion will be erased and I will forget every single memory of Hajj, then maybe my desire to go back to Mecca will regrow too, Insha Allah. Now, I consider that our hardest hajj is not the one in Mecca; it is the one of every day. If it is not right to judge a religion by its people, you know, we still have to live with them.

The First Day of the Rest of My Life
Michaela (Aminah) Cooper

Part of the beauty of embracing Islam is the 'story'. Almost everyone has one – short, long, humorous…. melancholy. Inevitably, at one time or another, you're asked, pleaded with to share your 'story': how did you come to Islam?

Well, ironically over the 20 years since I came into the folds of this blessed deen, I've yet to put my story into writing. Yes, I've told it many times; but, the irony is that I am a writer at heart, and yet have not felt compelled to write it down- until now.

I was raised a practicing Catholic, attending Catholic school from grade one. I vividly recall being not only an inquisitive child but a chatty one, as well! This explains my 2nd grade report card, with its 'F' for the religion mark ('F' standing for 'fair' back then). Amidst the 'E's' and 'VG's' (excellent and very good), the 'F' just didn't quite fit in. Could it have been the endless doubts and questions hurled at the unprepared nun teaching the concept of the trinity? Or was it perhaps my aversion to the common practices drilled into us regarding the Catholic faith and beliefs? Whatever it was, all that is left to show of my resistance to the Catholic teachings is that lone 'F' from Holy Name and my 'story'.

My beautiful, fascinating mother was blessed with five daughters. I, the youngest, and my oldest sister, Nadirah, both embraced Islam *alhamdulilah*. My sister had become Muslim ten years prior to my reversion, and although she wasn't directly responsible for the knowledge that ultimately opened my heart to the truth, her actions and that of her family instilled in me a deep respect for the commitment to their faith.

I still feel as though it were yesterday when I received a phone call from a relative who had met some Muslim brothers peddling incense and oils on the streets of Washington, DC. This relative was given the phone number of one of the brothers, and she called to see if I was interested in hearing what he had to say about Islam. Knowing only the basics from my sister (food, clothing, some *halal* and *haraam*), I was intrigued to indeed find out more.

She phoned the brother on a 3-way line, so I could listen in. I could tell he was only too delighted to have not one, but two as an audience. Interestingly enough, I became even more convinced that he had it all wrong. Despite my deepest issues regarding the trinity over the years, and all the confusion that it entailed, I still remained loyal to my faith. Why? Most probably because my time hadn't come to know the truth from the deception. So, there began my mission to 'convert' him back to Christianity! That phone call lasted approximately four hours and my relative ended up falling asleep on us that night, never to speak with the brother again.

However, I had many long, in depth conversations with this brother - a few of which were quite heated - until finally I agreed to take some literature to read and tapes to listen to about Islam. I honestly found myself in a struggle after reading the literature. In addition, our conversations became such that I was not only impressed with his knowledge of Christianity versus Islam, but the sheer notion that perhaps all these years I could have been wrong sent my life into a complete whirlwind. The struggle came in the fact that every letter of what I read about Islam, was very easy for me to believe. I began to feel as though I was betraying my faith (not to mention losing the battle to convert the brother!)

So I counteracted my new, but confused, feelings and asked for information about the Prophet Muhammad (peace and blessings of Allah be upon him). I believe the Prophet's life and teachings (peace and blessings of Allah be upon him) to be the key to my enlightenment. After reading about his life and struggles during his prophet hood, I was albeit ready to turn away from disbelief in the Creator, Allah…and grasp hold to what I believed was indeed the most amazing gift to mankind – Islam. Only two questions remained: Was I willing to make the sacrifices necessary to receive this bounty? And which 'Islam' would I follow?

Let me explain: Ultimately, there had come a point in my search where I informed my sister and her husband of my interest in Islam. It was actually at that point that I became even more confused. The confusion stemmed from the differences between what this brother was saying about Islam, and what my sister and her husband, Isma'il, were teaching me about Islam. I had much respect for my brother-in-law and sister, yet I couldn't distinguish the truth from the falsehood.

I recall another 3-way conversation, where I sat listening to my brother-in-law and this other Muslim brother exchange very opposing, and at times fiery, speech about Islam and its teachings. I remember thinking, with tears streaming down my face, "If there's this much hatred between the Muslims, I'm not sure I want to be a part of that!" But Alhamdulillah, Isma'il gave me very sound advice: "pray about it", he advised. He made it crystal clear that what I was indeed blessed with was the truth - but the message giver was just following a misguided form of Islam. He and my sister both wanted to desperately save me from this individual and show me his errors - but I had to learn it for myself. As for the sacrifices, the only thing that I wasn't sure of was whether or not I could manage the head covering (sheer conceit!) The brother offered me a beautiful reminder: "If you truly believe, you don't want to die in a state of disbelief…we just don't know how long we have in this life".

Alhamdulilah, I write this today as a Muslimah who adheres to the Qur'an and Sunnah as understood and practiced collectively by as-Salaf as-Salih. In the final days that led up to my taking shahada, I prayed harder than I think I ever prayed in my life. I spoke directly to Allah and asked Him to please clear up the confusion, and guide me to that which was going to grant me and my daughter heaven. As I was a single mother at the time, I knew this decision would affect not only my life, but also the future of my cherished offspring.

My prayers were answered when I simply awoke one morning and, upon looking into the mirror said, "I'm not a Christian if I don't believe what they believe. Indeed, I must be a Muslim because I know Islam is the truth, and I don't want to die as a disbeliever." I anxiously made arrangements to go to the mosque, and later that day informed my sister that I had taken shahadah.

My story...the first day of the rest of my life.

The Long Walk Home
Anisa Abeytia

I grew up in the shadow of downtown Los Angeles where streets are lined with rows of palms that turn and stretch, reaching for heaven. But I was raised on the wrong side of the Los Angeles River - the predominantly Latin Eastside. Yet, I did not have one ounce of "Mexican" in me. I was misplaced, malformed as I walked those streets with my cello in hand, passing by *taquerias* (taco stands) patroned by bald- headed *cholos* (hoodlums). I always knew it was summer because the neighbourhood smelled like pot and all the *cholos* were out of prison. I was a foreigner here, a tourist who took up permanent residence

I did not speak Spanish and no one ever believed me when I told them I was Mexican. Most people thought I was a Middle Easterner or Polynesian, so I began to believe the same. I had to be something different, since I did not fit in anywhere else. My name, Anisa, is an Arabic name that my mother thought she made up, a further enigma to my identity that made me forever foreign.

My only solace was my relationship with God. I talked to Him day and night. I told Him all my problems. I knew one day I would find a place where I would fit in and be accepted.

I was raised a Catholic like so many other Latinos, but I really believed. The problem was, I did not know what I was following, and I just followed. My mind was like water. I flowed in any direction and absorbed whatever someone placed in it, and like water, the universal solvent, I could cut through rock. Many times my head was as thick as rock and most of the time I had no idea what I was doing.

When I turned 19 I stopped attending church, not even for Christmas or Easter Mass. I was ashamed because I felt I had disappointed God. I was not growing up to be the person I always wanted to be, but I still really did not know who I was. God was always there for me and now I would not even visit Him in His house.

By this time I had fallen into a deep depression that would not loosen its grip on me until over a decade later. I did not sleep at night and would stay awake begging for God's help. All I could do was wait for a reply. The approach of night filled me with terror because I would have to endure another night alone. Dawn for me was a huge release that allowed me to dream. Even though I was so depressed, I was so grateful to God for the dawn because "verily with every difficulty there is relief" (Qur'an, 94:6).

I began to doubt God's mercy, not because I thought that He had let me down, but because I had let Him down. I did not feel I deserved His mercy and was abandoned.

That evening I decided to kill myself. I told myself it could not be worse than what I was living. I went out for a walk to the park near my house and sat. I was hoping if I stayed there long enough, someone would come and kill me so I did not have to do it. No one did, so I walked home, slowly. On that walk home I told myself how to do it, why to do it. I repeated it over and over until I was convinced. I was going to do it. When I reached my driveway, out of the corner of my eye, I saw something's faint flicker in the night sky. I looked over at it. It looked like a star, but I never noticed it before, I was quite familiar with the night sky by now. It began to move, so I assumed it was a helicopter. I started to turn away when I was forced down to my knees as this light came closer and closer. The next thing I knew, I was in my bed, in my pyjamas and the morning light was pouring through my window. I never doubted God's mercy after that and I knew He would never abandon me. I did not find out about Islam until a few years later when I was an undergraduate at the University of Southern California.

My journey to Islam was a culmination of many events. My name for one, and my appearance, attracted many Muslims to me at that time. I was like a magnet. They e-mailed me and sought me out in crowds. Even students I was tutoring began to ask me questions about Islam. This was all very strange to me. Stranger yet, my advisor encouraged me to pursue Islamic Studies. I later found out he thought I was Pakistani. It was at his request that I began to study Islamic philosophy, although I did not pursue a degree in that field. I was not seeking another religion, so conversion was the last thing on my mind. Despite my huge misgivings, I was happy as a Catholic.

I was happy until I began to read the works of the Church Father's (Bishops who produced influential works that were used for centuries) in Latin. When I read about the Trinity and the Council of Nicea, the scales fell from my eyes. I felt betrayed by my family and the Church who always said the Trinity was divinely revealed, but there I was, with the documentation. I said to myself, "you would not accept a counterfeit of Shakespeare's work, so why a counterfeit work of God's?" I could not be a Catholic anymore and the last thing I wanted was to be a Muslim.

I read *The History of God*, by Karen Armstrong. The author, who is not a Muslim, basically authenticated the life of Muhammad (peace and blessings of Allah be upon him) and the Quran. This was really something big, a historically accurate religion. I still did not want to convert, but I was interested. I asked myself, "so you consider yourself educated, then even if Muhammad (peace and blessings of Allah be upon him) wrote the Quran, it is a brilliant piece of work, so why not follow a brilliant thinker? "

It was not until I read the Yousuf Ali translation of the Quran that I realized that man had no hand in its creation. Just from a literary standpoint, it is unique. I was so moved by the text that I found myself needing to convert. I knew this was the real deal and if I let it pass me by, I was going to be in for it. I converted the next day, a Friday and that was in 1997.

I never did find my people or acceptance, but I found something more important - me.

Eventual Embrace
Jamal Orme

"I envy you," said his sister. "I wish I could believe in God."

He was embarrassed by her words. She didn't know that his faith was as yet unsteady, an infant stumbling into his first steps; momentarily up and then unceremoniously down again.

Yet, too sincere to preach piety, he scrambled for a suitable look to wear in silence, and found one of broad sympathy. As to who was the more deserving of sympathy at that very moment, he couldn't be certain.

"After all," she added, "you must really believe it. No one would choose to be Muslim," she reasoned. "If they didn't really believe it, I mean."

"Mmm," he nodded, knowing exactly what she meant.

* * *

"Can I ask you just one question," said the Moroccan, yanking at the gear stick with a crunch as they sped down the hill into Willesden. It sounded more like an instruction than a request.

"Yes," he replied, fearing the worst. But where could he go to, other than his destination? Afterwards he would feel that he had known the question before it was asked.

"Did you become Muslim for a girl?"

What had given it away?

Who was he kidding? He knew it. No one who looked like him would become Muslim. His driver on this chilly November night – a total stranger, tasked by the imam with taking 'this new brother' home – knew it as well as anyone.

He wondered if the imam himself had known it, as he clutched his hand for the shahadah.

He wondered if the well-wishers had known it, as they smiled at him and presented him with his new name – one he was sure he would never use.

"No," he replied, trying to sound convincing. This was no time for honesty.

The Moroccan was silent, and the silence was torment.

Before long they arrived at Kingsbury, never to see one another again.

* * *

"Don't blame me," she told him, lighting up a cigarette. "I didn't tell you to become Muslim."

It was true: she hadn't. And, at the outset, when it had first dawned on him that they would have no future together without Islam – in its outward form at least – he remained nevertheless certain that he, of rational mind, could never succumb to such a reduced existence.

Then the twin towers tumbled, and the turbulence began, and he felt frightened of these fanatics, mindful of his mortality. Would his life be concluded, one day on a tube train – no chance to say goodbye? What would follow? Why should one be troubled by such thoughts, when the conclusion of his careful life had always remained so distant?

But he had *not* been careful, he reflected ruefully.

He had fallen into something, and its floor fell further from him with each expiring day. When he contemplated climbing out, his heart tightened, for her.

For her, but… what else had he begun to feel? He remembered the sentence. Every word of every book she had given him, he had let them all wash over him – except those few.

"If man believes that he was not created, purposefully and by design, he must conclude instead that his life is entirely *without meaning*."

It had ingrained itself upon his mind, like a code, the comprehensibility of its implications tantalisingly within reach; yet for the moment, teasingly beyond his grasp.

* * *

When Abdullah asked him about his journey, he told him only about the sentence. He let it speak for him. He was scared to say more. Muslims who frequented the mosques seemed, to him at least, '*holier than thou*'. Those who had 'reverted' to Islam, holier still.

He returned the question to Abdullah, glad to push the spotlight away from his own story.

"I was always looking for God," smiled Abdullah calmly. "I always believed in God. I just needed to find Him."

"Where did you find Him?"

"Everywhere. In everything. All of the time. But when I found God in the Qur'an, that was when I became sure."

He was jealous of Abdullah's story. The beauty, simplicity, sincerity of it would have wiped his conscience clear, would have removed his feeling of being an imposter.

The way Abdullah glided through the mosque, he attracted no particular attention: enviably invisible. Yet, whenever he smiled, or spoke, Abdullah *belonged*.

It bothered him, and he disliked himself all the more for that. But why should *he* be the one to own the imperfect story, the one to have trodden the muddied path? Would God accept anything other than the complete sincerity of Abdullah?

* * *

He stayed away.

Stayed away from the mosques, from the Muslims.

Months passed. His first had been a wintery Ramadan; he had fasted as an exercise in self-discipline, and found that he could do it; but it was a lonely affair, and his Eid day flirtation with London Central Mosque was to be his last visit for some time. He hurried away at the conclusion of the prayer, uncomfortable to see such indiscriminate hugging. It implied brotherhood, and he was not a member.

And as those months passed, he distanced himself from his testament of faith – that memory which weighed so heavily upon him. At the same time, the phone calls of concerned brothers from that day gradually slowed to a trickle, and then stopped altogether. He was relieved; it was unnatural for anyone to show so much interest in one they did not know, and altogether inconsistent with the reaction he was used to: the looks of surprise when he entered a mosque, the brisk reply – "*Wa'alaykum*" – on some of the few occasions he dared to offer *salaam*. It was quite possible, he reasoned, that any who were stiflingly welcoming might be angling at recruiting him for pursuits he cared not to contemplate.

Only Abdullah persisted. It was awkward; she was suspicious of their friendship.

"Off to see your mosque buddies, are you?" she spat disdainfully on more than one occasion.

He tried to find excuses to avoid meeting, but found instead that he was hopeless at saying no. He acquiesced, trusting Abdullah more than the others. His Englishness was reassuring.

They met about once a month. It was uplifting, in a way he could not have foreseen. He still wrestled with the irresistible reality of the sentence, and Abdullah seemed to embody meaningfulness in his words and deeds. He would return from those meetings feeling almost positive about his predicament.

Once, a brother called Ishaq joined them. He was a friend of Abdullah's, born and raised a Muslim, and was intrigued by anyone who had chosen to join the faith.

When asked, he told Ishaq only of the sentence; but the weight of concealing his past, and his present, had become too much. When Ishaq departed, he confided in Abdullah all that had remained unsaid.

Abdullah listened patiently. Finally, he spoke.

"Your path to guidance is your path. It is not the same for everyone."

"But what if God thinks – or *knows*, I should say – that I'm not genuine?"

Abdullah was quick to respond.

"Do you fear Allah because of an imperfection in your belief?"

"Yes!" he replied emphatically.

"Then, if you fear Allah as you say," reasoned Abdullah, "ask yourself this: how could it be possible that you *don't* believe?"

He pondered this, and to his astonishment, realised that it was true. His faith had crept up on him unnoticed; so occupied had he been with the shame of his situation in his own eyes, and of how he feared others would perceive him, he had been oblivious to the quiet strengthening of his conviction that God was, indeed, The Truth.

When he looked back in later years, he isolated that moment, sitting cross-legged on Abdullah's living room floor, as the point at which he truly embraced Islam.

In the days that followed, still doubting that he would be regarded as a genuine Muslim, and wondering how that might affect his opportunities to marry, or to perform pilgrimage, he returned to the mosque and asked for a certificate of his reversion.

"I did my shahadah last year," he informed the shaykh.

"If you want me to certify this," he was told, "please say the shahadah again."

Without hesitation, he gripped the shaykh's hand and repeated the words; first, uncomfortably, in Arabic, then in English.

"I bear witness," he said with relief, "that there is no god but Allah."

"And I bear witness that Muhammad is the messenger of Allah."

An American Police Officer Discovers Islam
Linda D. Delgado

My Search

Twelve years ago I was fifty-two years old. I was not a member of any Christian church, but all my life I had been searching for the truth about God. I attended many churches and studied with their teachers. All fell short and I recognized none satisfying my quest for the truth. Since I was nine years old, I had read the Bible every day of my life. I cannot tell you, over the many years, how many times I searched it for the truth.

During the long years of my search for the truth, I studied with many religious faiths. For over a year I studied two times a week with a Catholic priest, but could not accept Catholic beliefs. I spent another year studying with the Jehovah Witnesses and did not accept their beliefs either. I spent nearly two years with the LDS (Latter-Day Saints, i.e. the Mormons) and still did not find truth. I had a Jewish friend and we had many discussions about the Jewish beliefs. I went to many Protestant churches, some for months at a time, trying to find answers to my questions.

My heart told me Jesus was not God but a Prophet. My heart told me Adam and Eve were responsible for their sin, not me. My heart told me I should pray to God and no other. My reason told me that I was responsible for both my good and bad deeds and that God would never assume the form of a man in order to tell me that I was not responsible. He had no need to live and die as a human; after all, He **is** God.

So there I was, full of questions and praying to God for help. I had a real fear of dying and not knowing the truth. I prayed and I prayed. I received answers from preachers and priests like, "This is a mystery" or 'You need to have faith and stop doubting what we teach." I felt that God wanted people to go to heaven so He wouldn't make it a mystery as to how to get there, how to live life accordingly, and how to understand Him. I knew in my heart that a lot of what I had been told and taught was not true or only half-truths.

I live in Arizona, USA and at the age of fifty-two had still never talked to a Muslim. I, like many Westerners, had read much in the media about Islam being a fanatical religion of terrorists, so I never researched any books or information about Islam. I knew nothing about the religion.

My Discovery

At the end of the year 2000 I retired after twenty-six years as a police officer. My husband also retired as a police officer. The year before my retirement (1999) I was still a police sergeant/supervisor. Police officers worldwide have a common bond, which we call a law-enforcement brother-sisterhood. We always help one another no matter what police department or country.

That year I received a flyer asking for help with a group of Saudi Arabian police officers who had come to the United States to learn English at a local University and attend a police academy in the city where I live. The Saudi police officers were looking for homes to live in with host families in order to learn about US customs and to practice the English that they would be learning.

My son was raising my granddaughter as a single parent. We helped him to find a house next to our home so that we could help in raising her. I talked to my husband and we decided that it would be good to help the Saudi police officers. We felt it would be an opportunity for our granddaughter to learn about people from another country. I was told that the young men were Muslims and I was very curious.

An Arizona State University Saudi interpreter brought a young man named Abdul to meet us. He didn't speak any English. We showed him a bedroom and bathroom, which would be his when he stayed with us. I liked Abdul immediately. His respectful and kind manner won my heart!

Next Fahd was brought to our home. He was younger and shyer, but a wonderful young man. I became their tutor and once they began to learn the English language we shared many discussions about police work, the USA, Saudi Arabia, Islam, etc. I observed how they helped each other and also the other sixteen Saudi police officers who came to the USA to learn English. During the year they were here, I came to respect and admire Fahd and Abdul for not letting the American culture have any impact on them. They went to mosque on Fridays, said their prayers no matter how tired they were, and were always careful of what they ate and always had excellent manners. They showed me how to cook some traditional Saudi foods and they took me to Arab markets and restaurants. They were very kind to my young 9 year-old granddaughter. They showered her with presents, jokes and friendship.

They treated my husband and me with respect. Each day, they would call to see if I needed them to go to the market for me before they went to study with fellow Saudi officers. I showed them how to use the computer, and I ordered Arab papers online and began to search the Internet to learn more about Muslims living in the Middle East and their customs and religion. I did not want me or my family doing anything which could possibly offend them.

One day, I asked them if they had an extra Qur'an. I wanted to read what it had to say.

They sent to their embassy in Washington DC and they got me an English translation of the Qur'an, tapes, and other pamphlets. At my request, we began to discuss Islam (they had to speak English and this became the focus of our tutoring sessions). I grew to love these young men, and they told me I that was the first non-Muslim they had ever taught Islam to! After a year, they completed their studies and training at the police academy. I was able to help them with their police studies, as I had been a police instructor during my career as a police officer. I invited many of their brother-officers to the house to help with university projects and to practice English. One brother had his wife come to stay here in the US, and I was invited to their home. They were very gracious and I was able to talk to his wife about Muslim dress, prayer ablutions, and similar things.

A week before "my foster sons" Fahd and Abdul were to return home to Saudi Arabia, I planned a family dinner with all their favorite traditional foods (I bought some because I didn't know how to cook all of them). I purchased a hijab and an *abaya* (long Islamic gown). I wanted them to go home remembering me dressed appropriately as a Muslim sister. Before we ate, I said *Shahadah* (public declaration of faith). The boys cried and laughed and it was so special. I believe in my heart that Allah sent the boys to me in answer to my years of prayers. I believe He chose me to see the truth by the light of Islam that shown from Fahd and Abdul. I believe Allah sent Islam to my very home. I praise Him for His mercy, love and kindness to me.

My Journey in Islam

My Saudi boys returned to their homeland about a week after my reversion. I missed them greatly, but was still happy. I had joined the local mosque as a member almost immediately after my reversion and registered myself as a Muslim. I was anticipating a warm welcome from my new Muslim community. I thought all Muslims were like my Saudi boys and the other young Saudi officers whom I had met and spent time with during the previous year.

My family was still in a state of shock! They thought I would stick with this new religion for a while, become disgruntled, and move on to another religion as I had done all my adult life. They were surprised at the changes that I began to make in my daily life. My husband is a congenial man, so when I said that we were going to be eating halal foods and eliminating haram (forbidden) foods, he said, "Okay." This was much harder than I had anticipated because I didn't know about many of the restrictions as far as slaughtering and checking labels to see the content to be sure there weren't harmful products in the foods. I was fortunate that my husband was not a fussy eater and that my family had grown use to me changing our household when I was searching for the truth.

My next change was removing pictures of people and animals from the rooms in the house. One day my husband came home from work to find me placing family pictures that had once hung on the walls in our home, in large, handsomely-bound photo albums. He watched and didn't comment.

Next I wrote a letter to my non-Muslim family telling them about my reversion and how it would and wouldn't change our family relationships. I explained a few of the basics of Islam. Still my family kept their own counsel, and I continued to work on learning prayer and reading my Qur'an. I got active in sister groups on the Internet and this facilitated my learning about my new beliefs.

I also attended a "Fundamentals of Islam" class at the mosque when I could get away from my work. I was still a state police sergeant and it was difficult – no, impossible to cover. This became a source of real discontent and concern for me. Just eight months and I could retire, so I asked for, and was granted, the right to telecommute from my home three days a week doing planning and research projects.

After the first six months had passed, sisters at the mosque that I attended still hadn't warmed up to me. I was disappointed. I began to feel like an outsider. I was puzzled and concerned. I tried to become active in community services with a few sisters who had been friendly toward me. I looked for the kindness, friendship, and best of manners that were practiced each and every day by my Saudi boys. I made many mistakes at the mosque, such as talking in the prayer room as I tried to get up and down from the floor. I went to a community celebration and ate with my left hand; I wore clear nail polish on my trimmed nails and got scolded. I did *wudu* (ablutions) incorrectly and was frowned at. I became very discouraged.

Then one day I received a package in the mail from a sister-friend who I had met on the Internet. In the package were several abaya, hijabs, silk stockings, and a warm and friendly note welcoming me as her sister in Islam. She lives in Kuwait. Next a dear sister sent me a prayer robe and prayer rug she had hand-made herself. This dear sister lives in Saudi Arabia. I got an email that had a statement that I always remember at times when I get that "outsider" feeling. The note said: "I am glad that I became Muslim before I met many Muslims." This is not an insult. It was a reminder that Islam is perfect and it is we Muslims who are imperfect. Just as I have shortcomings, so may my sisters and brothers. I also began to understand what I personally believe to be one of the greatest gifts that Allah gave to the Muslims: the sister and brotherhood in Islam.

Over the past twelve years my life has changed dramatically. My family has come to accept with generosity and tolerance that I am Muslim and will remain Muslim. All thanks be to Allah for sparing me the trials of so many reverts who must deal with beloved family who strive to dissuade them from Islam.

Gradually, I made some sister friends locally and by cyber space, dozens of sister friends became my Muslim family providing me with support, love and friendship. It was close to my first year as a Muslim that I became ill with a series of life-threatening diseases. I clung tight to the rope of Islam and was grateful for the black seed tea and ZamZam water that my sister-friends sent me from around the world along with their daily *du`aa'* (supplications).

As my health continued to fail and I grew weaker physically, I had to discontinue community service work and became more isolated from the local Muslim community. I continued to work hard on my prayer, having great difficulty with the Arabic pronunciation but not giving up. My Islamic teacher made some cassette tapes, and a sister brought them to my home to help me. After two years, I had learned to recite four *Surahs* (chapters) of the Qur'an. This may seem like a small number to most Muslims, but for me it was a very big accomplishment. I set about learning the words for the other parts of prayer, another two years of struggle.

I suffered a heart attack and had heart surgery. Prior back injuries I sustained in my past employment caused my spine to give me many problems making walking and movement painful. It was a sad time for me, as I knew that I would never again touch my head to the floor when praying, but would forever have to sit in my chair and pray. It was at this time that I truly understood the provision from Allah that Islam is the religion of ease. Praying while seated in a chair is acceptable; not fasting when one is sick is acceptable. I did not have to feel that I was less a Muslim because of these circumstances.

After visiting several mosques and observing that they were like mini United Nations, I began to see that the small groups within the mosque were mostly formed because of language and culture and not because of liking or disliking any person. I felt good that regardless of these differences, I could always count on a smile and an *"As-Salaam' Alaykum!"*

After a while, I began to gravitate towards sisters who are reverts to Islam like me. We have much in common – we experience many of the same trials, such as non-Muslim family members, difficulty pronouncing Arabic, being lonely on Muslim holidays, and not having a family member to breakfast with during Ramadan. Sometimes our reversions meant losing life-long friends who just couldn't accept our reversions, or it was because of our discontinuance in activities common to non-Muslims, such as dancing and mixing in groups.

As I have grown older and suffered two more heart attacks I have become mostly homebound. I began to search for some way to contribute to the greater Muslim community. I continually asked Allah for His help in this. One day, my young granddaughter suggested that I write books about my Saudi boys, Islam, and my family's experience with Islam. I decided to write the books and also include stories about a friendship group of Muslim and non-Muslim young girls. The stories I wrote included the young girls' problems and challenges they encountered at school and at home. I incorporated island by showing how it is relevant today. I wrote funny, creative, non-preachy stories I began calling "Islamic fiction". I continue writing Islamic fiction and promoting Islamic fiction today!

Next I created an e-group for sister authors and aspiring writers and this developed into the creation of the Islamic Writers Alliance Inc. The Alliance is a USA based non-profit organization for Muslim professionals and was created to provide support for Muslim authors and aspiring writers. The primary purpose of the IWA is to promote literacy worldwide and a major goal is to promote Islamic fiction books. Members strive for professional excellence and help each other promote their work to readers and publishers.

I decided that I would spend profits from book sales to buy books for Islamic children's school libraries. I discovered that many such libraries have lots of empty shelves where Islamic books belong. In 2005 I decided to develop and open my own book publishing business to publish other Muslim writers and their Islamic fiction stories.

I will always have much to learn about Islam. I will never tire of reading the Qur'an and one of my favorite pastimes is reading about prominent, historical Islamic figures. When I am unsure about something in Islam, I look to the Sunnah of the Prophet (peace be upon him). I see how he responded to situations and use this as my guide. My journey in Islam will continue, and I look forward to many new experiences. Daily, I thank Allah for His Mercy and Love.

I Rediscovered Islam
Nancy E. Biddle

I rediscovered Islam - although I had heard about it on various occasions all my life since nine years old - through music, culture and language. The Montreal International Jazz Festival invites world musicians to the festival. I was exposed to African music, Haitian music, and other bands from Europe and South America but it was the bands from North Africa and the Middle East that completely enthralled me: I was fascinated by the blends of the flat toned Arabic music with the sharp toned Western music and bought many cassette tapes.

I am not one to leave an interest lying on the surface. When I latch onto something I have to know everything about it. I was a musical novice actually! I hardly knew about my own Western musical influences like Classical, Rock, Jazz, Country, or even Folk much less Eastern varieties. But, suddenly, I was impassioned about music and so I dug deeply into Arabic music -and occidental music - with the convenience of the Internet. I had recently joined the Internet with a free AOL account and so had the world at my fingertips. I was also not working much at the time so had ample opportunity to explore both Classical and Modern Arabic music styles.

I added to my AOL and Yahoo public profiles "interests in Arabic Music". I learned the Arabic expression for hello, *marhabah*, and added that to my profiles too. This invited many Middle Eastern and French Speaking Arabs to chat with me. I asked them about mixed Western and Arabic music styles, and discovered Rai (Algerian pop music). I delved into culture and history, and the language, and the food, of course! I also discovered I could practice French in chat rooms from France and was frequently singled out by French speakers from North Africa for private chats. I learned an alternate expression for hello, "*Salaam' Alaykum*" and added that to my profile.

My conversations stayed pretty well within the boundaries of music and culture, but one day, an AOL user from Morocco "morooccanboyz" introduced himself to me and asked if I was Muslim. I said "No way! I am just interested in the Music and Culture." To the "no way", he responded, why not? And I did not have an answer! I was embarrassed to not have an answer about why I would not join that mysterious religion. The media's sensationalized answers did not seem to cut it for me. I replied, "Give me a few days and I will give you the real answer." It was then than I latched onto everything Islam.

Conveniently 80% of my French chat friends were Muslim and, like I had used them as resources to learn more about music, I used them too regarding Islam, and they were very happy to accommodate. As I read through sites about Islam when I had a question, I fired it off to them and amazingly, the answers all came back the same! This never happens in Christianity, or rarely. This was the biggest thing that impressed me, the uniformity and simplicity of the message and the facts about the faith taught equally across all the multi-national adherents.

During that time I just so happened to get more invitations out of nowhere to learn or discover about Islam. For example, I got an AOL invite to become friends with AOL user "convertstoislam" and I accepted the friendship and went to their site and read all the articles. I was referred from there to other sites, like whyislam.com, and a few others. I also tripped on some anti-Islam sites, both Christian and Jewish based and was glad for the "balancing of views" they provided. One site was about the thirty days of Ramadan, a Christian based movement for international prayer and activities to engage with Muslims to teach them during that spiritual month about the Saviour and the Truth. Unfortunately at the time (not so now) it was one of the best resources for learning about the Muslim faith. In fact, many of the anti-Muslim sites provided clear and easy to understand facts about Islam (although many now also include inaccurate information about Islam). I also say "not so now" because, since Islam has been in the spotlight due to various "terrorist" branded media exploitations, many excellent *dawah* sites have opened up *mashallah*. But at the time I was looking, not many quality sites were available in English or French.

It surprised me how, through all I read, whether about Jihad, or gender equality or rigorous defense of Islam, there was nothing not to like. I became convinced; Islam is Peace, the *tawheed* is the best message, gender issues are western interpretations only, Muslims love their religion and their Prophet Muhammad (peace and blessings of Allah be upon him) and defend Islam passionately with their life. I returned to "Morrocanboyz" with an answer "There is no logical reason why not!" But I did not say the *shahadah* at that time. All I had done at that point was open up the possibility that I could take on Islam whereas before I had never felt invited. I only needed to believe in Prophet Muhammad (peace and blessings of Allah be upon him), which would take some more research.

It is interesting to point out that when I came to decide that there was nothing stopping me from becoming a Muslim, I had not even experienced the Quran! At least not in English. Through my music explorations I actually had hit upon some "chanting" which turned out to be recitations and was of course drawn to the sound. I already knew about the Adhan and Ramadan and Hajj because of my exposure to it as a kid growing up in Singapore and as a teen living in Jakarta, but while in those countries I remained inside the Expatriate communities just observing the locals but it never occurred to me I could become a Muslim. Once we visited one of the largest Mosques in Indonesia, in Jakarta, and while there, a fellow who had just finished making *wudhu* in the "pond" in front attempted to take my purse when I was not looking. It seemed a bit of a downer at the time. We just laughed it off as it takes all kinds to make a world.

So that's the way it had been. I had always stood on the outside looking in. Islam was another peoples' religion, people who wore sheets, prayed in rows, fasted for an entire month, and went to Mecca in thousands and who spoke foreign languages, and ate spicy food with their fingers on mats on the floor. Now having arrived at "maybe I too can be a Muslim", I saw other whites who were Muslim, so I started to think of myself as Muslim too. At least, I adopted some of the outward practices like modest dress (I threw out all my skimpy clothes and went shopping for long-sleeved and loose fitting outfits,) diet (in the absence of halal shops, stopped eating meat, especially pork and bacon), manners (reduced encounters with men, looked down, experimented with covering my hair) and prayer (contemplation moments five times a day.) Like at a boutique, I tried it on to see how it fit. Deep inside I discovered that I have been a Muslim all my life, I just never knew it. The fit was perfect! I had also read up more about the proofs of prophethood and how they applied to Prophet Muhammad (peace and blessings of Allah be upon him) and became convinced he was a prophet of God and that Essa was a Prophet too. I saw that Islam believed in all the prior prophets and messengers and mentions of them in documents about Islam resembled the ones I had learned about in Sunday school. I decided that it was the right time to become a Muslim with the witness of my AOL friend, Moroccanboyz, with whom by email I made a date to meet on the coming Tuesday when he was off work.

That Tuesday came and went. Something happened in New York on that fateful Tuesday, September 11, 2001 that delayed my adventure. Whereas I had come to my decision to be a Muslim because it was something exotic to do, despite the truth of the message, despite the spiritual crises I had had in my Christian faith surrounding the authenticity of the scriptures about Jesus as the son of God and Islam providing an answer to that issue which cooled my soul, despite my new admiration for the Prophet Muhammad (peace and blessings of Allah be upon him), my whole reason for becoming Muslim was thrown into turmoil.

At first I hated everything to do with it, then when I calmed down I latched onto finding answers for why Muslims would be involved in that kind of event. Actually, it was my admiration for the faith and convictions of "terrorists" that were said to have executed the attack they must have held in their hearts to have followed through, however awful was the deed, with what they believed in so passionately. But how did they get so far off course?

It was then I discovered Quran translated into English. My version played an MP3 of the Arabic recitation line by line with a written interpretation underneath. I opened the first chapter, a short seven line, what seemed to be like a prayer; a paragraph, and I listened to it repeatedly more than thirty times. Finally I understood everything, including my place in Islam, contained in the last three lines about the paths.

I took my *shahaddah* online in an AOL chat with a brother from Saudi Arabia called WiseArab. He found me because he was looking to interview about the after effects of the 9-11 event that had happened two weeks prior. Already the news was reaching the Muslim world that North Americans were converting to Islam in droves. His cousin in Boston had desperately called him to help send Muslim books and resources to give the new Muslims a start; the Mosque was all out and orders were backlogged. It was completely incredible to him and he just wanted to find out how this was happening. However when he first popped up with a conversation approach, he said hello, and asked how I was. I said I was trying to join Islam but was not sure how. He coached me on the ritual words and I typed it out word phrase by word phrase. Done. That was it! I was now a Muslim. I asked what brought him to meet me and he mentioned the mercy of Allah, and explained his mission. During the chat he went to Amazon and ordered up a few books I would need, got my delivery information and said I'd get my order in ten days. He got my phone number and promised to call me and help me to pronounce the *Fatiha* for the prayer. After the chat I closed the computer, threw a sheet over my head and prayed the only way I knew how: to go into *sujud,* sit up, and go back. I was so overjoyed I cried. I even kissed the ground where I put my forehead.

A few days later as planned WiseArab called me and patiently helped me to memorize the *Fatiha* and pronounce it more or less correctly. The Saturday prior the fateful Tuesday I had actually seen a *Muslimah* on the bus and I had gotten off to follow where she went. She lived in a house a few streets up from mine. I did not bother her then because she was with a handicapped boy but I took note of the house number. After I declared my *Shahadah* I remembered her and left a letter in her mailbox asking for help, which she ignored for reasons Allah knows best. I was pretty well alone in Montreal. I knew no Muslim soul at all. And the white or black lid headed, red chequered cloth headed men, and women in scarves that I occasionally did see in the public transportation system disappeared from view. I found a Muslim school in the phonebook and my friend drove me there but it was boarded up with metal bars and was not at all open or welcoming. So that ended my attempts to link up with local Muslims and I fell back to relying on my Internet friends. A week later I received the books WiseArab had sent me and I was well on the way to living my new religion.

I need to say that some of my Internet friends rediscovered their Islam. After watching and witnessing my own transformation they realized that even though they were born into Islam, so that was their religion because it was the way they were raised, they actually had not chosen Islam yet. Some of them had actually left Islam because that was the only choice they saw to do - practice it or choose to leave it. Suddenly they all realized that they actually had the choice to choose Islam, and so many did!

Glossary

abaya – This is a generalized word used to indicate the outer over-garment worn by many Muslim women. In actuality, the Arabic word *abaya* means any over garment worn by either men or women, but for simplistic reasons for the mainstream public, it has come to indicate that which is worn by women when going out in public to cover her clothes she wears in the privacy of her home or in company only of close family and/or other women.

adhan – This is the vocal chanting of the call to the prayer performed audibly for each of the five prayers daily, and also for the special eid (holiday) prayers. The chant itself consists essentially of the words stated in the *shahadah* (declaration of faith), and also another statement encouraging people to attend the prayers in congregation by reminding them of the prosperity gained by this act.

ahadith – This is an Arabic term, the plural form of "hadith". The word hadith literally means story or relation. However, in terms of Islamic nature, it means specifically the collections (from various well-known and reputed scholars) of the sayings, traditions and life-style or even history of the life of Prophet Mohammed, peace and blessings upon him. In addition to the Quran, which is the direct word of Allah, the collections of ahadith are also referred to as the source of guidance for Muslims in all aspects of their lives.

Alhamdulillah – This word/phrase translates to mean "thanks to Allah (God)" or "praise be to Allah (God)".

As-Salam 'alaykum – This is the traditional greetings of peace used by all Muslims to one another, regardless of their own individual languages. Literal translation of these words is: "peace upon you". It is commonly used as both a greeting and farewell when parting. As with all other Arabic words and phrases which are transliterated into English lettering, there exist various different spellings of this same phrase.

as-Salif as-Salih – Literally translated, these words mean: "the good ancestors". It is in reference to the early generations of Muslims who came immediately after the companions of Prophet Mohammed (peace be upon him) and their followers.

aya – Literally translated, this word means "sign" or "proof". It is therefore understandable how this word is also applied to meaning "verse" when speaking of the Qur'an. It is commonly seen in various forms, such as "ayat" or "ayaat", indicating the plural.

Bismillah – This word/phrase is indicative of the introductory invocation for all things. Literally translated, it means "in the name of Allah", and it is a phrase/word that all Muslims are taught from the earliest days to say as an invocation of seeking blessing at the beginning of anything that is done. Upon opening a door, one says 'Bismillah', upon opening a can of food, one says 'Bismillah', and upon commencing to recite from the Qur'an or even upon commencing the prayer or upon commencing the ceremonial wash in preparation for the prayer, one says 'Bismillah'. Verily, at the beginning of everything and anything, one should seek Allah's bounty and blessings by remembering His name and His power with this phrase/word.

dawah – Literally, this word means 'calling' or 'preaching'. In terms of Islam, it means calling others to Islam, or simply spreading the news and truth about the religion.

deen – This word means 'religion'. In terms of Islam, it inevitably indicates the religion of Islam.

dhikr – This is in reference to the remembrance of Allah. For Muslims this remembrance is a form of worship of its own right, separate from the prayer or other forms of worship. In fact, 'dhikr' is done at specified times or places within the formalized prayer.

du'aa – Literally speaking, this is a method of prayer, or supplication. However, different from the more strictly regulated five-times-daily prayer that the Muslims attend to physically, this type of prayer attends to merely the spiritual side of the being. It is the method of direct communication between the person and his/her Creator with no intercessor or mediary in between. A du'aa, or supplication, may be recited during the regular scheduled physical prayer, or it can also be offered at any time of the day or night, and in essentially any place (other than places of defecation or similar unclean areas).

Fajr – This is the first prayer of the day, to be performed at a time when darkness remains, slightly before the actual break of dawn. There is also a chapter of the Quran given this name. The other prayers throughout the day and night are: dhuhr (noon-time), asr (mid-afternoon), maghreb (onset of sunset), and isha (night prayer approximately 1 & 1/2 hours after sunset).

Fatiha – This is the opening chapter of the Quran, consisting of 7 verses. It is also many times affectionately referred to as 'the mother of the Quran', or the 'seven exemplary (verses)', do to its high level of respect in Islam as containing within its seven verses the very essence of the teachings of the whole Quran, and it is in itself a prayer. Hence, the directive to Muslims to recite this chapter in every standing session of the prayers of every day.

garam masala – A mix of ground spices commonly used in the cuisine of Northern India and South Asia. Although sometimes used alone, it is also used in unison with other single spices. Although it is pungent, it is not necessarily hot with the nature of chili spices. A typical Pakistani Punjabi version of garam masala will include: black & white peppercorns; cloves; malabar leaves; mace blades; black & white cumin seeds; black, brown & green cardamom pods; nutmeg; star anise; coriander seeds.

hadith – Literally, this term refers to speech or a story. In terms of the religion of Islam in particular, it refers to various collections of direct reports from eyewitnesses handed down through the generations via reliable narrators, of the practices, traditions, speech and actions of Prophet Mohammed (peace and blessings upon him).

hajj – Literally speaking in language terms, this word means to travel or immigrate. In terms of Islam, it refers to the annual pilgrimage of all Muslims from all over the globe to one specific place at one specific time each year. Historically, the tradition of the various rituals practiced during the hajj is traced back to Prophet Ibrahim (i.e. Abraham, peace upon him).

halal – This Arabic word refers to things that are of the permissible nature.

haram – This Arabic word refers to things that are of the prohibited nature.

hijab – Literally speaking, this word means to hide or conceal something behind a protective curtain. In terms of the religion of Islam, it refers to the style of dress that the believing women adorn, in that she covers herself from head to foot in a concealing (i.e. non-revealing) manner. That means that her outer garments should be of such material so it is not sheer to reveal what she is wearing (or not wearing) underneath, it should be loose so as not to reveal the size and shape of her body excessively, and it should be of a bland nature so as not to attract attention to her. Many people tend to use this word in reference only to the headscarf that the Muslim women adorn.

imam – Literally speaking, this Arabic word means a leader of the people. It can even indicate a general of sorts. In terms of the religion of Islam, it refers to the leader of the prayer. In most cases, a masjid (i.e. mosque) will have only one imam and one muadhin (someone who announces the call to the prayer). However, for more populated mosques such as the haram of Makkah or Madinah, there are many men who are appointed and carry out the duty of imam (and muadhin), although of course only one will lead the prayer at any one given prayer time. Sometimes, for the longer prayers which are performed in the nights of Ramadan, one imam will lead for a portion of the prayer, while another (or numerous others at intermittent timings) will lead the prayer for the other portions.

iman – This Arabic word means faith.

InshaAllah – Although this looks like one word, it is actually a phrase made up of several words coming together as one. It means literally "as God wills", or "if God wills". It is customary to say this at any time of stating one's intention of doing something any time in the future, whether it be after several days, months or years, or only within several moments. The very act of saying this upon stating one's intention or desire to do something or see something get done is an act of worship, because it emanates one's faith in the power of God, that He indeed has power over all things, and that without His permission, nothing can be achieved, no matter how hard we ourselves try.

khutba – This Arabic word means the sermon given at the time of prayer, and in particular that sermon given on Friday or the two days of Eid celebration.

leban or laban – This Arabic word literally means buttermilk, but many people use it interchangeably as milk.

Madinah – This Arabic word literally means "city". However, in relation to Islam and in the world since the advent of Islam, it means that city in what is now known as Saudi Arabia, the city where Prophet Mohammed (peace and blessings upon him) and his companions (may Allah be pleased with them) migrated to in the early years of Islam, to set up the first true Islamic state, as they were chased out of their home of Makkah by their tribesmen who rejected Islam.

mah-shi – Literally speaking, this Arabic word means anything that is stuffed. In terms of food, it means stuffed food, and more specifically it refers to the variations of stuffed vegetables, such as zucchini, bell peppers, tomatoes, eggplants and potatoes, which is fixed in a stew-like preparation, filling the vegetables with a mixture of ground meat and rice with onions, tomato paste and spices.

marhabah – This Arabic word is known to Arabs of all regions, and is non-religious in intonation. It is a means of greeting another person, and is translated literally as "Welcome", but is often used as a simple "Hello". The meaning of this word, and how it is used, is a living example of the truly historical hospitable nature of Arabs in general.

MashaAllah – This is another instance of something which looks like one word, but is actually a phrase made up of several words put together into one. Similar to "InshaAllah", it also indicates the will of Allah, but in this instance it is said at times when one notices or hears of something admirable or attractive. Not only is it a way of the admirer to express his/her admiration for something, it is a means by which to ward of any harm coming to the owner of the admired quality or thing via jealousy or evil eye. Prophet Mohammed (peace and blessings upon him) has told his companions that the evil eye and affliction caused from jealousy is indeed real, and so he also advised that the person observing something he/she admires should say this phrase to ward off any possible harm coming to the owner of that quality or thing.

Mecca or Makkah – This is the city in what is now known as Saudi Arabia, in which one can find the Grand Mosque which houses the kaaba (square building) in the center, the direction in which all Muslims worldwide face for their prayers. It is the city in which Prophet Mohammed (peace and blessings be upon him) was born, and the city in which he received the first revelation of the Quran, and the city in which the message of Islam began.

methi leaves – The leaves of the Fenugreek plant, used as an herb in cooking, particularly for regions of the Indian subcontinent. The seeds of this same plant are often used as spices, again, in cooking particular to the same region. It is also a popular spice and herb used often in Ethiopian and Eritrean cuisine.

muadhin – This word is taken from the root "adhaan", and means the person who recites or announces the official call to the prayer of the Muslims (which is, in effect, the statement of the words of acceptance of faith, or the declaration of the faith of Islam).

naan – A leavened, flat oven-baked bread popular in South and Central Asia, including Iran, the Indian sub-continent, and the Persian Gulf states. Although it is most generally thought of to have originated from Iran, it is commonly known as a main side accompaniment to many dishes of Indian and Pakistani origin. Unlike the pita bread, it does not have the trademark 'pocket' quality. Also unlike the pita bread, naan is usually made of white flour only, of course combined with yeast, salt, water and yoghurt for the desired dough consistency, and set aside to rise before baking in hot oven.

pita – A round, flat leavened bread common to middle eastern and Mediterranean cuisines, the trademark quality of which is the inner pocket surrounded by the two sides of thin soft crust. This bread is equally good made of plain white, solid brown or a mixture of brown and white wheat.

raka or rakaas – A "raka" is one unit of the physical prayer of Muslims, in which one must stand for a period during which he/she recites specific verses from the Quran, then bows while still standing for a short period to recite specific words glorifying Allah, then stands again for a short period during which one can recite a short remembrance of Allah, and then prostrates to the ground, putting forehead and nose directly on the ground for a short period during which the worshipper again glorifies Allah with specific words, then sits for a short period during which a specific supplication is recited, then prostrates a second time with forehead and nose to the ground during which words glorifying Allah are recited again. All of this action makes up one unit, or "raka" of the prayer. Then after completing this, the worshipper should either stand to perform another raka, or if this is the last, then they should sit to recite more words of remembrance and specific supplications and then officially close the prayer with the words of peace repeated over each shoulder, beginning with the right and then the left. The word "rakaas" is simply the plural form.

Ramadhan – Although there is strong indication that the people of Arabia used this word for this particular month of the calendar before the onset of Islam, it is most strongly known for its association with the religion of Islam as the month in which all Muslims in all areas of the world fast during the daylight hours for the entire month. In addition, it is the month in which the first revelation of the Quran was delivered, and the month in which the most important of the early battles between the Muslims and the disbelievers occurred in the early years of the history of Islam.

sabr – This Arabic word means "patience". When you tell a person simply "sabr", it is like saying, "have patience with me".

salaam – Literally speaking, this Arabic word means "peace". As it is the essence of the phrase which Muslims use to greet one another (Assalaamu 'alaikum), many Muslims will basically shorten it to "salaam" at times when greeting one on repetitive occasions coming and going within frequent occurrence of one another, or in extremely familiar settings. Although this is widely accepted by many Muslims to shorten the formal phrase to this short word, it is still better and comes with the promise of greater reward if one uses the formal phrase or even another longer version of the same thing.

salat or salah – This refers to the physical formal prayer of the Muslims.

salla llahu alayhe was salam – This is an Arabic phrase, literally translated to mean: "prayers of peace and blessings of Allah be upon him". According to traditions and practices of Muslims, it is said or written immediately after the mention of Prophet Mohammed by name. Because different people write Arabic words, names and terms in English lettering in different manners, it can many times be found spelled slightly differently, such as: "salla Allahu alaihi wa sallam", or other similar spellings, but it means essentially the same thing. Also, in many English language texts, authors will revert to simply translating it into the English equivalent, such as: "peace and blessings be upon him". Depending upon the differences of writing preferences of individual authors, this phrase is also sometimes represented in shortened format of letters depicting abbreviations of the words, i.e.: "saw", "saaw", or "pbuh".

shahadah – This Arabic word literally means "witness". In terms of the religion of Islam, it means the words to be said to confirm one's declaration of faith.

shaykh – Literally speaking, this generally refers to someone of advanced age. It is also a term of endearance used in reference to someone in position of the society which commands respect of others. In terms of the religion of Islam, it means someone who leads the people by giving them sound logical advice based upon the teachings of the Quran and sunnah. This term is also used in reference to teachers who teach the religion to the people. The word 'Shayukh', or 'Shayookh' is merely the plural form of this word.

Subhan Allah – This is another instance of a phrase which appears as if it is one word. Actually it is several words put together as one, hence actually a phrase. Literally translated, it means "Glory be to Allah", and is stated at times when it is proper and fitting to glorify Him.

suhur – This Arabic word means the meal taken before the break of dawn and before performing the fajr prayer in the early morning hours, hence the meal taken before commencing the fast of the new day.

sujud – This Arabic word means the position one is at for the prostration of the prayer, in which one is on hands & knees, with forehead and nose touching the ground, and hands on either side of the head. It is in this position that we are promised that Allah will not only hear, but also answer our calls upon Him, therefore we are advised to increase our private supplications while in this position.

sunnah – This Arabic word is in reference to the traditions, practices and even the speech of Prophet Mohammed (peace be upon him).

surah – Literally, this word means "picture". In terms of the religion of Islam, it means the chapters of the Qur'an.

tawheed – This word means the one-ness of Allah, and is the essence of all of the teachings and practices of Islam.

wa-alaykum – Literally, this phrase means "and upon you". It is the shortened version (which should be "wa-alaykum assalaam") of the return of the greetings whenever one is greeted by another person with the words of peace.

wudhu or wud'u – This word means the washing, or ablution, to be performed to ceremonially prepare oneself in cleanliness to face the Creator in prayer.

Zamzam – This is the name given to the well which miraculously appeared at the heels of baby Isma'il's feet, as his mother frantically went to and fro between the mounts of Safa and Marwa, looking for any sign of civilization or even mere life in the forlorn desert area in which they had been left by Isma'il's father, Prophet Ibrahim (Abraham, peace upon him). This well is still producing water until this day, and Muslims from all over the world partake of it whenever they visit the region of Makkah on their pilgrimage. It is a blessed water, as Prophet Mohammed (peace and blessings be upon him) said that the zamzam water is for what it is intended, therefore if one supplicates upon drinking, Allah graciously answers the prayer by causing the water to perform whatever duty (such as healing various ills of the body) which the worshipper supplicated.

Acknowledgments

Behind every book there are dedicated individuals who help to make a good book even better. Members of the Islamic Writers Alliance (IWA) who went beyond what a normal volunteer does and gave their time and professional skills to help make *Serving Up Faith: Recipes – Cooking Tips – Inspirational Stories* a very good book are thanked and acknowledged for their generosity.

Saara A. Ali – thank you for the work you did as the organization's content collector and organizer.

Balqees Mohammed – thank you for your beautiful cover art work and for the professional editing of the manuscript for this book.

Mahasin D. Shamsid-Deen – thank you for your content editing work for this book.

Linda D. Delgado – thank you for serving as the cookbook project manager and book publisher.

Jamal Orme, Ivanka Khan, Aminath Shiyana Yahya, Maryam Funmilayo, and Amina Malik - thank you for serving as our content reader team.

Finally, many thanks to the IWA members who contributed financially to this cookbook project.

IWA Board of Directors 2011-2012

Linda D. Delgado, IWA Director

Mahasin D. Shamsid-Deen, Assistant Director

Balqees Mohammed, Secretary

Sabah Negash, Financial Officer

Pamela K. Taylor, Marketing Officer

Member Contributors

Abdul Rahman Mojahed is a translator, reviser and author. He was born in 1982, Damietta City, Egypt. He graduated in 2006 from Islamic Studies Section, English Department, Faculty of Languages & Translation, Al-Azhar University, Cairo, Egypt. He is the author of *Superior Woman, Inferior Man in Islam*, as the first in a series of books aimed at unveiling the truly pure nature of Islam. He is also the author of *Jihad: Peaceful Strife for Reformation*, which is still under publication.

Amel S. Abdullah is a freelance writer, editor, and Arabic to English translator of Italian-American heritage who embraced Islam in 1994. An avid cook, Amel believes that one of the best ways to learn about a culture is by experiencing its cuisine. Amel can be reached via e-mail at amel.abdullah@yahoo.com.

Amina Malik is a lawyer, freelance journalist and creative writer, residing in London, England. Amina's articles have been published in local and national newspapers. She has published fiction, non-fiction, and poetry in magazines, books and online publications. Amina's writer's website is www.aminamalik.co.uk.

Aminath Shiyana Yahya is a fun loving person who loves spending time with family and friends. She enjoys volunteering in order to help make a positive difference in the wider community. Her other interests include researching, writing, travelling, seeking self-understanding and understanding others, sketching, reading, music and films.Anisa Abeytia holds an M.S. In Holistic Nutrition from Hawthorn University, an M.A. in Literary Theory from Stanford University and a B.A. in Creative Writing (Poetry and Fiction) from the University of Southern California. Since 1999 she has studied and researched health, healing and natural living and studied to become a Certified Islamic Healer. She attended the oldest herbal school in the U.S. Anisa writes on topics of health and nutrition and contributes regularly to various magazine and online sites worldwide, specializing in thyroid and endocrine dysfunction. She is the author of over fifty articles that were translated into five languages. Currently she works with clients worldwide and maintains the website, www.womens.healingcircle.org.

Balqees Mohammed, author, editor & graphics designer, draws upon her gained experience of 30 years as a Muslim and her life in Saudi Arabia, representing some of that in her recipes of this collection. Originating from the US and a non-Muslim family, she enjoys sharing with others the experiences she has witnessed. A collection of her articles on Islamic Awareness can be viewed on her blog at: www.balqees59.wordpress.com. For information about her editing services and other works, view her website at: www.writers-consultant.com.

Christine (Amina) Benlafquih writes on varied topics including religion, food, health and culture. You can find more of her recipes on the web at Morrocan Food at About.com (http://morrocanfood.about.com).

Dr. Freda Shamma focuses on developing curriculum and curriculum materials for Islamic full time schools. She is the co-author of *Ayat Jamilah: Beautiful Signs: A Treasury of Islamic Wisdom*, with Sarah Conover at www.noorart.com. Her newest work is an Anthology of Muslim Literature: 750-1250 C.E. She lives in Cincinnati, Ohio.

Ivanka Khan is a freelance writer and editor. A member of Society of Children's Book Writers and Illustrators, Islamic Writers Alliance, and Travel Writers Association, she is most passionate about children and travel writing. She graduated with a degree in International Business and Middle Eastern Studies from SJSU, California. She currently resides in Dallas, TX.

Jamal Orme reverted to Islam in 2002. A teacher by profession, he taught in mainstream UK schools in London, as well as two Islamic primary schools. He has also worked as an education advisor in the United Arab Emirates. Jamal had his first novel, *The Victory Boys*, published in 2011. It is available at the IslamicBookstore.com. Web sites: http://thevictoryboys.com.

Judith Nelson Eldawy is an American Muslim with a background in nursing and eclectic interests. Her Egyptian in laws have finally come around to eating her cooking since she no longer tries to tempt them to taste "weird" international dishes like mac and cheese or salad with lettuce. Judy is the 1st place winner of the 2010 Islamic Fiction Stories contest sponsored by the IWA annually.

Linda D. Delgado is the owner-publisher of Muslim Writers Publisher. She is the author of ten books, most notable her award winning *Islamic Rose Books* series. She founded and is the Director of the Islamic Writers Alliance Inc. Her writing and professional work is focused on promoting literacy and Islamic fiction. www.muslimwriterspublishing.com and www.islamicfictionbooks.wordpress.com

Linda K. Jitmoud, also known as Jamilah Kolocotronis, is a native of St. Louis, Missouri who converted to Islam in 1980. She is the author of six novels and one non-fiction work. Her books include the five-book *Echoes Series*. Jamilah currently lives in Lexington, Kentucky with her husband and youngest sons.

Mahasin D. Shamsid-Deen, author, poet, educator and playwright. Assistant Director of IWA for five years and member of International Women Playwrights and African

American Women Playwrights. Has more than fifty published articles and often lectures on issues of Islamic fiqh. She is married with three children and enjoys sewing and trying new recipes. Web site: www.islamictheatre.com.

Maryam O. Funmilayo is an avid reader, a freelance writer, and a poet based in Raleigh, North Carolina. Striving to balance her temporary life on earth as a Muslimah, daughter, sister, wife, graduate student, and homeschooling mum to four kiddies, has been a life-long, challenging, fulfilling, and soul-inspiring experience.

Michaela (Aminah) Cooper is a seasoned, yet unpublished writer. She has been writing poetry and short stories since childhood. A teacher by profession, Michaela and her family currently reside in the United Arab Emirates, where she is also homeschooling her 4 children. Her passion is learning and studying the deen.

Nancy E. Biddle is an accomplished author and founding member of the Islamic Writers Alliance. She resides in Montreal, Quebec, Canada. After reverting to Islam in 2001 she settled down in Marriage. She has no children at the moment. Her birth name is Nancy Elizabeth Biddle and goes both by N. E. Biddle and by her Muslim name. She is an environmentalist, active member of several community groups and successful business owner.

Nazli Currim is a retired preschool educator of 38 years. She received her degrees in English and Psychology from the University of Karachi, Pakistan, and her Montessori Certification from Association Montessori Internationale. She holds a diploma from The Institute of Children's Literature, Domestic Violence 101, and has completed a 4 yr. course in Quranic Tafseer from Al Huda. Nazli enjoys art, books, languages, travelling, gardening, ikebana, writing, and helping with refugee work. She has two grown children and lives in Gilbert, AZ. Her first published children's book is, *Grandma Lives With Us*. www.nazlicurrim.com

Norma Kassim is currently a doctoral candidate doing research in philosophy and metaphysics of Islam. A single parent with six grown-up children and three grandchildren, she also does editing and proof-reading work which includes thesis and dissertation especially on Islamic subjects. She hopes to continue in the area of Islamic research work and also write books. Published work: *A Walk Through Life*: issues and challenges through the eyes of a Muslim woman. Blog: www.annckay.blogspot.com

Saara A. Ali is a librarian turned homeschooling mom and blogger. At her site, Ummah Reads (http://muslimkidsbooks.wordpress.com), Saara writes about books for children and teenagers and how families can make reading a part of everyday life. In her spare time she enjoys writing short stories for adults and stories for children.

Sabah Negash is a teacher by day and a writer by night. She writes children's stories, poems and curriculum aides for use in home schools and Islamic schools. She loves to cook and try out new recipes and reinvent old ones. Sabah can be reached at familyreads@ymail.com and www.worddiaries.blogspot.com.

Soumy Ana is a freelance writer who writes articles for ehow. She has written two young adult novels, *Salam Bullies* and *Islamdale 3000, The Mosque of the Future,* as well as many short stories. Soumy Ana is the winner of the 1999 IWA Short Stories Contest. Her website is located at http://soumyana.weebly.com/

Umm Juwayrriyah is a twenty-something born Muslim woman of West Indian ancestry and a mother of two. She holds an Associate of Arts degree in Communications and she is currently completing her Bachelor's degree at Bay Path College. She is an elementary school teacher, the current editor for the New England Muslim Women's Association, a published poet, freelance writer, and the former assistant director of the Islamic Writers Alliance. Her first Urban Islamic fiction book, *The Size of a Mustard Seed,* was published in 2009. website: www.authorummjuwayriyah.com and Urban Muslim Writers: www.islamicurbanwriter.bravehost.com

Uzma Mirza is a registered and licensed green architect with ncarb; Leed certified with the US Green Building Council. Originally hailing from Canada, she is a founder of a green architecture consultancy and a non-profit charity, Pen and Inkpot Foundation, a published Islamic calligraphic artist, a writer and poet. Web site: www.aynarchitect.com (Architecture). Other Web sites: www.thepenandtheinkpot.org (Art) and www.pifdn.org (501c3 Philanthropy).

Wendy Meddour was born in 1975 and grew up in the quirky little seaside town of Aberystwyth. Following her love of literature (and the sea), she went to study English at Exeter and Cardiff University. She came away with a first class BA in English Literature, an MA and PhD in Critical and Cultural Theory and an irrepressible love of books. After a spot of lecturing, she took up a position at Oxford University where she spent eight happy years researching and teaching English. She is currently writing and illustrating her first series of children's books for France Lincoln. It's called *Cinnamon Grove* and is aimed at 8-12 year olds. Book I: *A Hen in the Wardrobe* will be out in Spring 2012, shortly followed by Book II: *The Black Cat Detectives.* Blog at: www.wendymeddour.wordpress.com

CPSIA information can be obtained
at www.ICGtesting.com
Printed in the USA
LVOW02s2300030517

533193LV00004B/42/P